Street Girls

Street Girls

Hope on the streets of Brazil

Matt Roper

Paternoster Lifestyle is an imprint of Paternoster Publishing,
PO Box 300, Carlisle, Cumbria, CA3 0QS, UK
and Paternoster Publishing USA
PO Box 1047, Waynesboro, GA 30830-2047
www.paternoster-publishing.com

British Library Cataloguing in Publication Data

A catalogue record for this book is available
from the British Library

ISBN 1-85078-403-5

Cover design by Campsie
Printed in Great Britain by
Cox and Wyman, Cardiff Road, Reading, Berkshire

Contents

Foreword

Bridget and I travelled to Bangladesh in January 2000 to look at the work of the aid agency, World Vision, in a variety of settings, and to meet the child we had sponsored for the previous five years. It was a memorable trip in very many ways, but perhaps the most moving experience of all was our visit to a street girl project in the centre of one of the worst slums in Dhaka. To see how these homeless, loveless, futureless little girls were being introduced to care, warmth, cleanliness, play, music and regular food was an enormous privilege and a great inspiration.

This book is about the way in which Signpost International's Matt Roper is helping to bring hope and healing to similar children who have spent their lives on the streets of a major city in Brazil. I would dearly love to visit the Meninadança project, where dance can replace drugs and prayer might replace prostitution, but, as I probably never will, it is enough to know that such a creative, comprehensive initiative exists, and that I can pray for it.

How wonderful to see that God is bringing together the power of art and prayer and sheer hard work. You will be inspired and amazed by the story of Meninadança. But that is not enough. Matt Roper dreams of a day when the streets will be empty of crack-addicted girls. The ways in which we as individuals react to this extraordinary story may bring that day a little closer.

Adrian Plass

Acknowledgements

Thanks to my parents, David and Eileen, for their constant support and understanding, I love you both very much. For being my sister, thanks Katy, along with brother-in-law Derek and my new niece, Emma.

Thanks to Kerry Dixon for being such a close friend and for always believing in me. Thanks to everyone at Signpost International, particularly Alwyn, Ray, Richard and Fiona. A special thank you to Richard Wallis, who is also my 'literary agent' (sorry about that time in Rio!). Thanks to Jeff and Becky Hrubik from PAZ in Santarém, and to Danny Smith of Jubilee Action.

Thanks to my 'second family', the Fosters, Penny for hot meals and waterbottles (amongst other things!), Allen for being my official guru, Katie for your inspiring faith. May my margarine tub always have a place in your fridge.

Thanks to the members of St John's Church, Mansfield, and St James' Church, Hemingford Grey. Thanks to all the other churches and groups in England, Scotland and Wales that support me. Thanks to all those individuals who support me and pray for me, or have donated to the project. Never underestimate yourselves – you really are helping to turn lives around. Thank you to some university friends who turned out to be my faithful supporters, especially Jenni, Judith, Sara, Hannah and Tim. Thanks to John Clucas and Spectrum Print, St. Ives, for your faith and generosity.

There are so many Brazilians I should thank that I am sure I will miss many of them out. To everyone at Meninadança, especially Warlei and Nahilla, Márcia, Cleber, Magali, Hamilton, Ana, Nilce, thank you for really 'vestindo a camisa', taking on the vision heart and soul. Thank you to the many Brazilians who have helped us in whichever way. Thanks to prosecutors Eduardo and Tânia for believing in our ideas and potential, and to Pastor Márcio of the Lagoinha Baptist Church, Belo Horizonte.

Thanks to my worship group 'Chamas', for being such great friends and brilliant musicians. Especially to Clay, Graziela, Natanael, Toninho, Mardoqueu, Daví, Vânia, Lídia, Miro, Daniel, Jody, Andréia, Susan, Tatiane, Eduardo and Rita. A special thank you to some special friends who have always been on my side, especially Isaias and Ruth, Orlindo and Sirlene. Valeu mesmo!

This book is dedicated to all the girls that are mentioned in its pages, and for whose cause I dedicate my life.

Thank You, Lord, for my walk with You.

1

Pylon Hill

'Juliana . . . Juliana, wake up!'

I gave her a gentle shake, but it was no use. It was 9.30 a.m., an unearthly hour for a street girl to be awake. Stretched out in front of Bob's burger bar, underneath a tattered blanket, 13-year-old Juliana was dead to the world, oblivious of the hurried, early-morning crowd that stepped over her or scurried around her ... I shook her again, and she began to stir.

'Juliana, wake up, please. You have to help me today.'

She opened her eyes for a moment, and quickly shut them again. The sun was dazzling.

'I need coffee,' she groaned.

'Hold on.'

I dashed over to a roadside snack bar, and bought a strong espresso and a doughnut. When I returned, Juliana was sitting up groggily against a 24-hour cash machine.

'Good looking, aren't I?' she heckled at some passers-by who were watching as she woke up. They looked shocked, and scuttled on. I crouched down at her side, and she took her breakfast eagerly.

'Thanks, Uncle,' she said.

'Juliana,' I began, 'Do you know where the girls are staying? I can't find them anywhere.'

It was causing me great concern. Most of the street girls were nowhere to be found as I walked around their normal haunts and hideouts. I had not seen some of them for months.

'They're up in Holy Mary, Uncle,' said Juliana, slurping her coffee. 'I saw them all last night. They passed by here on a stealing spree. They wanted me to go with them, but I wasn't up for it, so they left me here on my own. My sister's there in Holy Mary too. But, Uncle, you shouldn't go there. It's dangerous.'

I had heard of Holy Mary, a notorious *favela*, or shanty town, renowned for its violent drug wars. Its real name was Pylon Hill, after a cluster of electricity pylons that towered above it. It was a no-go zone for anyone but drug dealers and crack addicts.

'Will you take me there?' I asked.

Juliana seemed slightly perplexed. 'If that's what you want.'

I helped her up, and she folded her blanket neatly, hiding it underneath a nearby cast-iron manhole cover. I put my arms around her shoulders as she hobbled off, still stiff from sleeping on the hard pavement. It took an age to walk the short distance to my car, as she stopped at every coffee shop and snack bar to ask for freebies. By the time we reached the car, Juliana's hands were full of sweets, sticky buns and cigarettes.

'What are the girls doing in Holy Mary?' I asked as I pulled out. Juliana was still trying to make sense of the seat-belt.

'They're *noia*-ing,' she replied.

I remembered that street-kid slang. It came from the word 'paranoia', the sensation you feel when you smoke crack-cocaine. It confirmed what I had already suspected.

'How many of them are doing that?' I asked.

'All of them,' replied Juliana. 'At Holy Mary the *noia*'s cheap and easy to find. They stay until they've spent everything, then they go back into town and make more money, you know how . . .'

That explained why I was no longer finding the girls as I walked the city-centre streets. They had, it seemed, swapped their soaked rags of paint-thinner and pots of glue for something much more deadly, more addictive. I asked Juliana if she was also smoking crack.

'I tried it, but I didn't like it. I'm back to sniffing paint-thinner.'

I stopped at a traffic-light. Suddenly there was a television camera in my face, and a man with a microphone.

'How was your first snog?' he laughed. It was for some Saturday night TV show. I looked baffled.

'It was all right,' I replied.

The lights changed, and I drove off. It all seemed rather surreal.

Like most of Belo's slum areas, Pylon Hill is a stone's throw from the impressive apartment buildings of the city's richest. Sitting like an open wound between two of the city's slickest suburbs, it is a cacophony of jerry-built shacks and cheek-by-jowl, red-brick shanties, built precariously on a steep hillside.

I parked my car on the main road, and we walked a short distance, past a steakhouse and a BMW showroom, until we reached the busy entrance to Pylon Hill. A group of chattering women congregated, laden with bags of groceries. Toddlers played in the dust, chasing and shouting. Many others walked in and out, their shabby clothes and dark complexions giving them away as people of the *favela* as they mingled in amongst the others on the main street.

A group of bare-chested men lingered on the corner of one of the alleys that forked off, wearing oversized Bermuda shorts and neck-chains. As we walked past them, one muttered, 'What's your business?'

'He's with me,' retorted Juliana.

She took my arm, and led me through a maze of narrow alleys and tight passageways, guarded by scurrying rats and snarling dogs. On either side were crumbling brick walls or makeshift fences of wood and corrugated iron; behind them, the crying of babies, the smell of stewing beans, and the pounding rhythms of samba and pagode. The giant electricity pylons loomed overhead like the statue of a god.

We emerged at the top of a flight of concrete steps, and in front of the entrance to a house a large black man sat rigidly on a plastic chair. He had a shaved head, a scarred face and a hardened expression. He held a penknife in one hand, juggling it nervously between his fingers.

'This is Pedro,' introduced Juliana.

I guessed that he was one of the dealers, or maybe a look-out. I offered him my hand.

'What do you wanna buy?' he asked, abruptly. He had a deep, growling voice.

'Nothing, I . . . '

'He works with us, the street kids,' Juliana interrupted. 'He helps us. He's a good guy, and he's English.'

I was not too sure how advantageous it was to be called a 'good guy'.

'Ha, ha,' he boomed. 'You work with these little rascals, then? That's good.'

'It is?'

'Yeah. I can't stand to see these little kids stoned out of their brains. They're only children, aren't they. Well done.'

At that moment a small boy scurried up, with tangled hair, caked with dirt and barefoot. He unclenched his tiny fist, revealing a five-real note, which Pedro took and tucked into his Bermuda back pocket. He took his penknife, carved off a minute piece from a white ball, and placed it into the boy's waiting hand. The boy dashed off again, disappearing down the steps behind where Pedro was sitting.

He turned to me again: . . . 'You really shouldn't be here. It's very dangerous. The cops are always doing raids, catching us all by surprise. Sometimes they don't even bother asking questions; they just come in shooting. A mate of mine was killed here last week, just about right where you're standing. He was a good guy, just like you.'

I quickly stepped aside, and looked down. There were bloodstains on the cement floor. As I looked up I noticed a revolver tucked into the front of Pedro's baggy shorts. I was beginning to feel a little out of my depth.

'I'm looking for some of the kids from the streets. Do they come here?' I mentioned a few names.

'Well, you've come to the right place. We've got 'em all here, big ones, small ones . . .' Pedro was sounding like some dodgy salesman.

I asked him about the girls.

'The street girls? They're here day in, day out. Smoking one rock after another. They get completely out of their heads, smoke, smoke, smoke, until they've blown it all. When they've run out of money they sell their clothes, their earrings, anything. Then they start selling themselves . . . '

'Can I go in there?' I asked, pointing to the steps behind him.

'Go on,' he replied. 'But don't think they'll want to talk to you. They won't even recognise you!'

Pedro chuckled and turned his head. 'There's someone coming down,' he yelled down the steps. 'He's good blood. I don't want anyone messing with him, all right?'

I made my way carefully down the concrete steps, which were strewn with burned matches and drinks cans. I had heard of this place. It used to be a children's play area, built and proudly unveiled by the city council a few years before.

I turned a corner, and found myself in an enclosed area, a drugs den. A man lay keeled over on the floor at my feet. Groups of people huddled together in silence, engrossed in their cupped hands. Others slumped on their own, drawing on pipes or aluminium cans, or painstakingly preparing their next 'trip'. It seemed a desperate, tragic place.

'Arrghh! It's Uncle Matt!' came a sudden cry from the far side. 'How embarrassing! Don't come over here, please, Uncle!'

It was Fernanda, a 14-year-old girl from one of the gangs in the city centre. A few people raised their heads momentarily.

'So, here's where you are,' I called back. Fernanda covered her face with her hands. Her older sister, Patricia, sat next to her, along with two other girls, Bruna and Poliane, who were also 14. The four were always inseparable.

'Go away, Uncle,' cried Poliane. 'I feel so ashamed.'

I had known Poliane for a number of years, and just a few months earlier I had taken her back to her mother's house. She had desperately wanted to stay there, but ended up running away because her stepfather was beating her up. She had two broken front teeth.

Kênia was less bashful. She came running up, and hugged me.

'Oh, Uncle,' she whimpered. Kênia was a tiny 12-year-old, with matted Afro hair, who spoke with a pretend baby voice, her way of winning people over. Six months before, a policeman had smashed her in the mouth with his baton while she was sleeping in one of the city squares, and she had lost all her bottom teeth. She sighed as I stroked her head, and then went back to her smouldering pipe.

I spotted another girl that I knew, perched on a concrete slab. It was Jaqueline, Juliana's sister. She was 11, the youngest of the girls, and had a beautiful face and expressive dark eyes. On her eleventh birthday I had, to her delight, taken her out to an ice-cream parlour. Now she was gazing into space, motionless, her hands clasped tight.

I walked over, and put a hand on Jaqueline's shoulder. She turned her head, and looked at me. Those beautiful eyes were now empty, her expression vacant. She managed a feeble, 'Hi, Uncle.'

'What are you holding so tightly?' I asked.

Jaqueline unclenched her tiny hands, revealing three small rocks of crack.

'Oh dear, Jaqueline,' I said.

She looked at me again, open-mouthed, her lips broken and bleeding. Her body was so frail, sucked to the bone. She said nothing, but her deep brown eyes seemed to cry out, 'Help me.'

As I left Pylon Hill, I fought back the tears inside me. The odds seemed too heavily stacked against these tragic, beautiful children. What was I thinking, to have gone there, to have wanted to see it with my own eyes? I would never be the same again, I knew. I had to do something.

2

Too deep, too dark, too desperate

Pylon Hill's drugs commerce resembles Belo's bustling Sunday bargain fair. At every bare wall people huddle together, their hands cupped around their faces. On every corner of the *favela*'s narrow alleys, cannabis and cocaine are sold in tiny plastic packets. Crack is carved, like a kebab, from the 'rock', depending on the price. I used to joke with the dealers that they had mixed it with soap powder to make more money, which they probably had.

I began to go to Pylon Hill almost every day, and walk around the *favela*'s concrete maze. Entering the crowded drug dens, I would sit for a few moments with each of the girls as they lit up and puffed on their crack pipes. Some were too drugged to talk or even to listen, and sometimes I would not say a single word. But just being there was a way of showing that I cared.

It was after nightfall, however, that the street children would arrive in their hordes. They would pounce on women going home from work or students leaving night school, then straddle the back of the 9801 bus to Pylon Hill, spending their loot in an ecstatic instant. Then they would return to the streets, armed with a knife or a piece of broken glass, and an uncontrollable craving.

One night I sat at Pylon Hill's bustling entrance, observing each barefoot boy and girl as they leapt off the bus and ran excitedly into the shanty streets, clutching tightly their screwed up notes. Two policemen were posted on the main street, turning a blind eye to the constant coming and going.

'Uncle Matt!' came a cry from behind me. I looked around. It was Poliane, running down the cobbled *favela* hill towards me.

'Hey, Poli!' I shouted.

She took my hand and caught her breath. 'Uncle, the Gypsy wants to see you.'

'The Gypsy?'

'Yeah. She looks after me here. She says she's dying to meet you. Come on, she's waiting for you.'

I remembered hearing this name before. Many of the girls had also talked fondly about the Gypsy. One told me that she would give her food and a bed for the night. We climbed a

steep hill towards a silhouetted figure standing by an open door.

'So, you're Uncle Matt. I've heard so much
about you.'

The woman walked towards me and shook
my hand firmly. She wore a long, silken dress,
and an array of cheap over-the-top jewellery
that rattled whenever she moved.

'Nice to meet you, Senhora . . . ?'

'Gypsy. They call me Gypsy. You can just
call me Gypsy.' She spoke quickly and nervously, and her eyes were wild and darting.

'I've also heard a lot about you, Senhora
Gypsy.'

'Sure,' she continued, taking my hand.
'We're two of a kind really. We're both trying
to help these poor street kids, aren't we? I can't
bear to see the little mites sleeping out there in
the cold. My house is full of them. I just can't
bring myself to turn them away when they
knock at my door, all dirty and hungry. I want
to ask the council to give me some money so I
can open a house for them. Maybe you can
help me?'

'Well, maybe . . . '

'Come on in, please.'

She stepped through the doorway and into
a shadowy, musty room. There was a tattered
blue sofa, a three-legged wooden stool, and a
portable television balanced on an upright
wooden crate. At the far end, a curtain made

from strips of plastic sacks led into a further room. I gasped as I noticed a large black man, standing motionless in the corner by the door, his crossed arms bulging with muscles.

Looking down, I saw something even more disturbing. A small boy, no more than ten years old, crouched on a dirty rug on the floor, inhaling eagerly from a crushed Coca-Cola can, his other hand burning the top of the can with a cigarette lighter. I looked around at the Gypsy.

'I can't stand to think of them, smoking their rocks out there, with everybody else,' she explained, throwing her arms in the air. 'I'd rather they do it here, in my house. I look after them here.'

She made a gesture to the boy, who scuttled off behind the curtain. I wondered how she would word her proposal for council funding.

'Please, sit down.'

I sat on the edge of the mouldering sofa, and the Gypsy perched on her wooden stool. As she talked, children would knock on the door, push notes of money into her hand, and disappear behind the curtain. Some physically shook and sweated as they rushed in. I recognised one girl, Alcione, a 16-year-old who had been sleeping along with some others by a disused shop-front in the city centre. She stopped and hugged me.

'Oh, Uncle Matt, have you come to see me? You see, I've come off the streets! Now I'm living with the Gypsies. That's good, isn't it?'

I was beginning to see why the girls were so attached to the Gypsy. This tiny hovel was what is known in Brazil as a *fumodrome*, a safe house for smoking drugs, and one which almost always harbours other types of illicit activity as well. I wondered how, for example, the girls got the money they needed to buy their drugs; and why the street children the Gypsy was sheltering so benevolently were all girls. I worded my questions carefully.

The Gypsy, however, had gone into some kind of drug-induced trance and was getting increasingly difficult to understand. Dragging on a roll-up cigarette, she rattled on in Portuguese mixed with Spanish, her gestures becoming more and more erratic. I gulped as I noticed, on the floor beneath her stool, a six-inch carving knife.

'I really must be leaving,' I managed to interrupt.

'No, you mustn't go yet,' urged the Gypsy.

'No, really . . . '

'But it's very early to be leaving,' she moaned, her voice strange and altered.

Somehow I managed to jostle my way past the door and out of the Gypsy's house, making a dash for the main road.

'Come back here!' she shouted after me, her jewellery jangling. 'We haven't talked about the council funding!'

A few days later I returned to Pylon Hill, and found Juliana loitering at the entrance to the *favela*.

'What are you doing?' I asked.

'Waiting for my sister,' she replied. 'I can't go in there because I've run up debts, and I haven't got the money to pay. A guy got killed with fifty bullets here last night. He'd got himself into trouble with the dealers too.'

'I thought you weren't using that stuff.'

Juliana looked coy. 'Sorry, Uncle. I was ashamed. I lied.'

'How much do you owe?'

'Five reals. If I go in there I'm dead.'

Five reals - less than three pounds. Lives like Juliana's were worth nothing, I thought.

'I'm looking for Lorena. Has she been here?'

Lorena was a 12-year-old street girl that I had followed for a long while. I had not seen her on the streets for four months or more.

'Lorena? She's here all right. She's so *noia*-ed that she assaults cars at the lights here so she doesn't have to go too far. She stays down at the lower part of Holy Mary.'

I thanked Juliana and made my way into the shanty alleys. I had never been to the lower part of the *favela*, but I knew of its notoriety. I came across Pedro, who took me to the top of a steep flight of steps and pointed me on. His gang was 'at war' with the one that controlled the lower part.

'This is the point of no return,' he laughed. 'Good luck!'

Lorena was a beautiful and expressive girl with a horrific past. She had been beaten up and sexually abused by her stepfather from an early age. According to her grandmother, she sometimes used to arrive in her house unrecognisable from the severe beatings. Lorena's mother chose her partner over her daughter, and Lorena ran away to the streets, where she continued to be abused by the older street boys. The blows to the head, along with the heavy drugs she started using, seriously affected her mental health. On one visit to Lorena's home while she was living on the streets, I arrived early and found her stepfather, a duty policeman, alone in his shanty shack. He took his pistol and started waving it around, making disguised threats. 'Sometimes I lose control of myself,' he muttered, wielding his gun. 'I just don't know what I'm doing, and I end up doing something I regret.' . . . I wondered if he had ever regretted wrecking the life of his beautiful, young stepdaughter.

I could feel every staring eye as I carefully made my way down the steep muddy stairway. Women offered dope at the doors of their houses, in the same way that housewives from the upper part sold ice-lollies. A few youths watched me suspiciously, and as I passed by I complemented them. My heart was beating faster and faster.

Lorena was sitting upright against a brick wall at the bottom of the steps. She was puffing on a pipe made from a bent piece of plastic tubing, covered with aluminium foil. She was with another four grown-up crack addicts, each engrossed in their own 'trip'. I shook her gently by the shoulder.

'Lorena, I've been missing you.'

She looked up at me, her eyes glazed and yellow, and carried on smoking. She was just skin and bones.

'Lorena. It's me, Uncle Matt.'

This time, she turned her back towards me. She scrambled on the floor for any residue worth smoking. She was so drugged that she did not even recognise me. Lorena used to be such an affectionate, attentive young girl.

The climate was heavy, and I decided that I should not stay any longer. I began the steep ascent back to the upper part of Pylon Hill.

'Hey, mate. What are you doing here?'

I jumped as two youths with shaven heads appeared behind me. I quickened my pace.

'I work with the street kids,' I gasped.

'Don't kid us. You were here buying drugs,' one of them shouted from behind me.

'No, really,' I insisted. 'I help the kids here.'

Their tone was getting more aggressive.

'You can't fool us, mate. We saw you come down here with Pedro. He always shows people where to buy the stuff. Hand over your money.'

I had arrived at the top of the steps, and the two began to close in on me. I fumbled in my pocket for a letter that I carried from the Belo Horizonte Children's Court, officially stating that I worked with the street children; a friendly judge had written the explanatory letter to get me out of sticky situations just like this.

'Here, look at this.'

One of them took the letter and looked at it, and then ripped it up in front of me. It probably looked too official.

'You're a policeman!'

'No, I'm not!' I implored . . . That was the worst thing I could be accused of in a place like this. At that, the first made a grab at my watch, while the other tried unsuccessfully to snatch the chain around my neck. My watch strap broke, but I managed to grab the pieces, and began to run. The two youths took off after me.

Unsure of where I was, I ran for my life, ducking and diving through the *favela*'s narrow alleys, always aware of their chasing feet close behind me. At last I found myself on a road that I recognised, and made a dash for the busy entrance to the *favela*. My heart was pounding, and as I staggered onto the main street I was gasping for breath. The two arrived soon afterwards.

'You see him? He's a thief! He's been stealing from people in the *favela*!' one of them shouted, pointing towards me. All eyes were on me.

'He robs from you honest *favela* people!' bellowed the other.

Juliana, still waiting for her sister, came up to me.

'Go away, Uncle,' she pleaded. 'Don't stay around here any more. It'll just get ugly.'

I took her advice, and went to get my car. I had arranged to have lunch with two well-to-do Brazilian friends. I arrived late, my shirt torn and my neck scratched with nail marks. I had no choice but to tell them what had happened.

'Are you out of your mind?' they exclaimed in horror. 'You mustn't ever go into one of those *favelas*, do you hear? Promise us you'll never do a thing like that again!'

It took a week or so before I mustered the courage to return to Pylon Hill. It was following a distressed phone call from Sofia, one of the most experienced girls on the streets. She had reversed the charges.

'Uncle Matt, I'm pregnant. You have to help me,' she sobbed, before being cut off. I discovered that she had begun living with a 35-year-old drug pusher. She was only 14.

As I arrived, I met a group of street children who were leaving for a stealing spree, having smoked themselves skint. They told me how Lorena had been caught breaking into a house in the *favela* and stealing a hi-fi system in order to buy more drugs. She had been severely beaten up by a group of men, and pushed down a hill, nearly ending up dead.

I found the place where Sofia was living, in amongst a cluster of makeshift brick buildings. I had to haul myself up to arrive at the front door, as the house was high up and there were no steps. I knocked on the door, but there was no answer. I clapped my hands and called out, and someone inside finally stirred.

'Who is it?' asked a groggy voice.

'It's Matt. I'm looking for Sofia.'

There was a rattling, and the door swung open. It was Elaine, Sofia's older sister, her mop of hair a tangled mess.

'Come in, quickly,' she beckoned.

I stepped inside, and glanced around the murky room. Apart from a few dirty blankets sprawled on the floor, the house was completely empty. There was no furniture, no kitchen, and no bathroom, not even a light bulb. The whole place reeked of urine.

'Uncle,' Elaine began, lowering her voice to a whisper. 'Sofia left early. She's petrified. If she doesn't do what Tulio tells her, she gets a thrashing.'

'Tulio?'

'That's her husband. He's a monster. Last week he knifed a man to death.'

I asked if Sofia was carrying his baby.

'Yes, and he says that if she has an abortion, he'll kill her. She gets beaten up every night. You see that?' Elaine pointed to a puddle on the floor. 'Last night he beat her so badly that she wet herself there and then. She was screaming and crying.'

There was not one street child in Belo Horizonte that did not like Sofia. She was attractive and charismatic, a natural leader. She had run away from her family home in Governador Valadares, a city in the north of the state, when she was only six years old, because her drunken father used constantly to beat her up. She began living with a gang of street children next to Belo's bus station.

Her good looks made her natural prey for paedophiles. She would sell her body for a plate of food, or a can of glue. She moved from glue to paint-thinner to crack, and began assaulting shoppers in the streets, or motorists as they waited at traffic-lights. I would often meet Sofia as she dashed through the city centre on a stealing spree. As she became more and more addicted, she needed more and more money. Her 'marriage' to a dangerous drug pusher was just another form of prostitution, a way to feed her insatiable addiction. Later, I met Tulio in a bar near the house. I offered him my hand, and he showed me the barrel of his pistol.

'Don't come near my girl,' he growled.

Sofia quivered in the corner, too frightened to look up. The girl who would outsprint furious shopkeepers was now captive to a drug that would, sooner or later, kill her.

As I walked back to my car, I felt a deep sense of hopelessness, mixed with anger. The pit of despair into which these girls had fallen just seemed too deep, too dark, too desperate. Deep inside me I could feel God's heart breaking. The girls did not deserve this. They were just innocent victims.

That night I wept and prayed, my heart heavy and troubled.

'Lord, what should I do? I feel so helpless, so overwhelmed. But I know that you brought me here for a reason. Do something, Lord. Do it through me. But do it quickly. Time is running out for them.'

3

Walking in the clouds

It was like nothing that I had ever imagined. The heat, the dirt, the danger, the constant exposure to broken, seemingly irreparable lives. It was far removed from the life that I had wished for myself, or dreamed of. But it felt right.

With every individual that I came close to, living on the edge of death, snared by the deadly claws of crack, I felt somehow that God was there, ministering to me. As I listened to so many stories of shattered lives and shredded emotions, the love of God seemed to well up inside me, doing me so much good. It was something very profound.

I had never been in any way close to tragedy. I grew up in a loving and secure Christian family, a father and mother who bent over backwards for me. I was born in Mansfield, a Nottinghamshire town, once dependent upon coal mining, now trying for recognition as a Robin Hood tourist site - and not as one of the country's murder capitals, its other claim to fame. Despite the town having its fair share of social problems, my parents kept me well away from them.

Perhaps one of the only things that I failed to learn from my parents was their patient endurance. They were the only Christians in their large families, but never gave up praying. It was only after 30 years of prayer that one of my many aunts gave her life to Christ at the 1982 Mission England Crusade with Billy Graham. One by one, almost all of my relatives on my father's side came to know Christ. All from rough mining backgrounds, the change in their lives was radical.

My sister, Kate, is very much like my parents. After leaving university, she married and settled down, and gave birth to a beautiful baby girl. She is easy-going and not overly ambitious. We are very close, although very different.

From an early age I earned a nickname that stuck for most of my adolescence, Scatty Matty - or various forms of it. I was easily distracted, or, as my mother used to put it, I walked around with my head in the clouds. I certainly dreamed a lot. I wanted to make my mark on the world.

Apart from my family, two people particularly influenced my early life. The first was

Nick Harding, the leader of my church youth group, now a writer of Christian books and songs for children. It was through Nick's ministry that I first experienced God in a tangible way, on Pentecost Sunday 1986. The second person was Kerry Dixon, who arrived at my church, St John's, Mansfield, as a Church Army evangelist on his first placement. He was also a dreamer, and I much admired his enthusiasm and energy. Instead of quelling my dreaming, he encouraged me to dream bigger and more wildly.

At the age of 15, I decided how I was going to conquer the world. I was to be a pop singer. I played the piano and sang, imagining myself as a fresher version of my hero, Elton John. My school would let me out for a day a week to go and nurture my new-found passion in a local recording studio, subsidised by the county council.

A year later I 'released' my first album, a pretentious collection of deep and dreamy songs inspired by, among others, Sylvia Plath and William Shakespeare. John Cooper, a poetical friend, was my Bernie Taupin, writing the lyrics while I composed the music. We were both impossible to live with. I took the whole thing extremely seriously.

A little later my girlfriend dumped me. My teenage world collapsed but, in true artistic style, I let it all out in my music. Sobbing on my school's grand piano, I wrote a tragic love-song, entitled 'I Wish'. It went: 'I wish I'd found the words to say, there's a numbness deep inside I can't explain, but now it's too late.' It was enough to make anyone heave. I recorded the song and offered it to my ex-girl-friend, hoping that she would be filled with remorse and beg to come back. Instead, she played it to almost everyone in the school. It was extremely embarrassing.

I managed some good A-level results, and secured a place studying music at Sussex University. I decided, however, to take a year out, working with Kerry Dixon in the parish where he was now posted, in the tiny Cambridgeshire village of Hemingford Grey. While my job description was to assist Kerry in doing outreach from the lively village church there, I had other intentions for my gap year. It was to be my make-or-break year.

Hemingford Grey was very different from Mansfield. They don't tend to eat mushy peas and mint sauce in the market square. They use napkins on their laps at dinnertime. And din-nertime is in the evening and not at midday, which is lunchtime, and there is no such thing as teatime. I had a lot to learn.

Just outside St Ives, Hemingford Grey is a picture-postcard village, complete with river and quaint thatched cottages, and home to many doctors, solicitors and other well-to-do professionals. The village had fought on Cromwell's side against the Crown during the civil war. Now, however, they had to deal with Scatty Matty. I was a full-time worker in the church, and my chaotic enthusiasm left many people's heads spinning. I wore a dangly earring, and my hair was shoulder-length on the left side, and short on the right!

However, the church community was very gracious towards me, and continued to love and nurture me. The Fosters, who put me up during the year, became like a second family to me. I made many other deep and lasting friendships.

In the evenings and at weekends I would play and sing in the pubs and clubs around Cambridge and Huntingdon. I described my singing style as a mixture of George Michael and Demis Roussos, although a professional singer friend once likened it to an asthmatic whale.

I would sing every Sunday afternoon at The Territorial, Huntingdon. I kept one of their publicity posters, which read: 'Bring your mother to hear Matt Roper and have a steak'!

In the winter of 1992, Kerry asked me to go with him and a team to the Philippines. He had taken up an invitation from a Filipino pastor friend to visit some churches there. I was a little apprehensive, but being billed as a 'singer and international recording artist' tipped the balance for me. I raised the money I needed through my gigs in pubs and clubs. Although it was the first time that I had travelled abroad, I was sure that the culture shock would not be as great as my painful transition from the East Midlands to East Anglia.

My month in the Philippines was a turning-point in my life. I remember the lump in my throat as I came in to land at Iloilo City, and looked over the sprawling shanties, corrugated iron roofs and dusty tracks, which seemed to stretch out forever. I was completely taken aback.

The first time I walked the filthy city streets, I noticed a small boy, begging by the roadside. As I passed him, I was shocked to see that he had no arms or legs, and I asked my Filipino guide who he belonged to.

'Everybody knows about this boy,' he began. 'His mother was so poor that she sold him to a gang, for a few hundred pesos. The gang cut off his arms and legs, so that people would take pity on him, and they leave him here all day to beg. At night they come and take his money.'

I was aghast.

'There's nothing we can do,' continued my Filipino friend. 'The gang is very dangerous.'

I remember the precarious wooden walkways, balanced on stilts above stagnant water and raw sewage, where shanty children chased and leaped. I was invited into desperately poor houses, where a family of ten would crowd into a room much smaller than an average English bathroom. They would insist on buying me a Coca-Cola or a snack, a luxury that they would never have dreamed of buying for themselves. I felt so humbled by their generosity and faith.

It was something akin to being run over by a juggernaut. Suddenly, everything about me was put into question. My faith, too, did not seem relevant any more. I began to wrestle with myself and argue with God.

'Lord,' I would pray. 'Do you care about this? What do you have to say about it? Why don't you do something about it?'

One morning we were praying together as a team on the rooftop of the church building. Kerry laid his hands upon my head, and I fell to the floor, overpowered by God's Spirit. As I shook and wept, God used Kerry to speak His word into my life: 'You must make a choice. Me, or your music.'

It was a tough word and yet so full of love. God wanted to use me, but I was not letting Him. I had set for myself a different agenda, shutting God out. I was such a dreamer, but I had never let God in on my dreams.

As I recovered I said to God, 'There's really no choice. If you want me to give up my music, then that's what I'll do. I'm yours.' It is a prayer that I have had to pray many times since.

A few days later I was riding a jeepney, a brightly decorated army jeep and Filipino form of public transport. Opposite me there sat a Filipino trainee missionary from Manila's YWAM base, whom I had met briefly that morning and who would be leaving later that evening. As we bumped along the potholes in the sticky heat, I closed my eyes and tried to doze. When we got down at our stop, the young man took me aside.

'I don't know you well, but I have to tell you something,' he said. 'While you sat there, in front of me, I saw you in a vision. You were standing on a flat, empty plain. But you were looking down, underneath the earth. You could see what was going on underneath the surface, everything that was wrong, everything that was evil and unjust. One day, friend, you will be talking to powerful people, governments and leaders. God will use you to uncover injustice and speak up for those who have no voice.'

Back in England, I shared that vision with some friends, and then forgot about it. It was only after many years that they reminded me of that prophetic word. God's dreams for me were bigger and wilder than even my own.

The trip also had a profound effect on Kerry, who came back with an ardent desire to meet the needs of the Filipino church. We talked fervently about our experiences to friends at church, and began a small programme to sponsor needy children from the church where we had stayed. At first based in Kerry's spare bedroom, that humble initiative eventually grew into Signpost International, today a rapidly expanding children's charity working with local Christian groups in six countries.

I spent three reluctant years studying Music and Media at Sussex University, Brighton. The course content was based on modern, experimental music, and I spent many long hours devising weird and wonderful ways to play a piano without using the keys. In one piece which I wrote for five voices, the lead vocal sang by following a circular stave and reading a telephone directory. During a performance, the audience erupted in laughter when she warbled, 'Chicken Tandoori, eat in or take away.' Another piece, Concerto for Six Public Toilets, was a musical masterpiece of flushes and slamming seats, but not well suited for the concert hall.

At times I found the whole thing terribly pointless. We would spend hours eagerly discussing musical philosophies, going round and round in theoretical circles. My final year dissertation was pretentiously entitled, 'Music and the Repression/Emancipation of the Sensibilities'. Music, I argued, is able to free the oppressed masses. It got me my honours degree, but I did not believe any of it.

Once again, I had my head in the clouds. I could not forget those children, struggling to survive amidst crippling poverty, living by their wits on so many city streets. I pinched a Gideon's Bible from the university health centre, and began to highlight every verse relating to poverty and injustice. By the end, I could hardly believe the number of verses that had come up. As I flicked through it, the whole Bible glowed with bright yellow highlighter. I was convinced: God was on the side of the poor and oppressed. His heart broke with love and compassion as he looked upon so many lives, trapped in a deadly spiral of hunger and poverty.

I began to become involved with human rights issues and campaigning groups. I was president of the Christian Union, and we began to take part in campaigns about world debt, political prisoners, oppressive regimes and child sex tourism, among others. When the then Conservative government finally bowed to pressure, agreeing to change the law so that paedophiles who abuse poor children abroad could be prosecuted in Britain, we threw a party. We felt that we had managed it all on our own.

As I read about victimised children around the world, one story in particular broke my heart. It was an article by Gilberto Dimenstein, a reporter from the Brazilian newspaper *Folha de São Paulo*. He had travelled around the Amazon basin, uncovering an organised ring of child prostitution, where young girls were snatched from their homes and enslaved in brothels in remote mining towns. He even spoke of auction houses where young girls were sold to the highest bidder, the virgins fetching a higher price.

I did not stop to think, I was overtaken by a tremendous sense of urgency. I had to go to Brazil, I convinced myself. Although I did not know how I should go about it, I would not rest until I was there. It was incredibly naïve, but it came from the bottom of my heart.

I rushed to meet Kerry. Once again, he did not crush my dreams. Somehow, he convinced the trustees of Signpost International that they should pay for an impetuous young man to plant himself in the middle of the Amazon jungle. Six months after graduating, I was waiting on the tarmac at Gatwick airport, full of anticipation. I was off to save the world.

As I look back, I know I had not thought things through properly. All that I had was enthusiasm, which had often got me into a lot of trouble. I had no experience, no training, and little wisdom. I did not even speak the language. I was going to have to learn the hard way.

I remember peering out of the two-engined jet's tiny window as we turned and swooped down into Santarém, a small town on the banks of the Amazon river. The mighty rain-forest stretched out over the horizon, a carpet of lush green that seemed to cover the whole earth and bend with its contours. Below me, the colossal river moved slothfully on, to be met by another river, the Tapajós, whose black waters contrasted dramatically with the Amazon's murky brown. I could hardly believe that I had arrived.

From there, my journey has been exciting, unpredictable, full of adventures. It has also been difficult and fraught with pitfalls. There have been times of exhilaration, and times of great loneliness and frustration. I spent six months in the Amazon, before moving on to Belo Horizonte, a massive industrial city, 3,000 miles away from Santarém, and worlds apart from it.

Belo is Brazil's third-largest city, 200 miles inland from neighbouring state capitals, São Paulo and Rio de Janeiro. It was the first modern Brazilian city to spring from the architects' drawing boards, although its careful planning was quickly thwarted by mass migration from famine-stricken towns in the interior. Now, Belo Horizonte suffers from the same urban – social problems as Brazil's other metropolises: abject poverty on a massive scale on the hillsides and invaded land areas, alongside the equally exaggerated luxury of the city's upper crust. As always, it is the children who bear the brunt of Brazil's cruelly divided society.

Working initially with a local street-kids project, I began to visit the gangs of young children living rough on Belo Horizonte's city-centre streets. I would play card games, perform magic tricks, paint their faces and care for their cuts and bruises. They loved to play-fight with me, as I would swing them about in the air or roll around with them on the damp mattresses and dirty blankets. I would often leave the den filthier than the kids, which they thought was great.

The street children came to trust me, turning to me whenever they were in trouble or need-ing help. For them, I had become a member of the gang, an uncle, part of the street family. When one of the boys, addicted to drugs, stole a note from my wallet, he spent nearly two months in hiding, fearing reprisals from the other, furious gang members. They considered me a close friend, and the feeling was mutual.

After a year working amongst the street children in Belo, I moved again, this time to Rio de Janeiro, with the British human-rights group, Jubilee Campaign. There I researched and wrote a report on the murder of street chil-dren by extermination groups, entitled *The Silent War*. The 60-page report was launched in the British parliament, and reached the desks of influential Brazilian ministers. It also made a three-page, full-colour insert in a British daily tabloid, *The Mirror*, and a charity CD with a guest appearance by Paul McCartney.

However, I was unable to forget the street children that I had come to know and care for, so I returned to Belo Horizonte. I was especially concerned for the girls, who saw me as a father figure. They always turned to me when they needed help. I would answer reverse-charge phone calls well into the early hours. 'Uncle, it's me! I'm lost, I don't know where I am. Please help me!', 'Uncle, I've been stabbed in the back. I'm in hospital. You need to come and sign me out.'

Every day the girls were getting more and more deeply entrenched in street life, without anybody to extend a hand to them. Most worrying of all, they had stumbled upon a deadly drug, crack, which was quickly destroying their already fragile lives. Lost, alone, forgotten – but God loved these tragic girls, I knew. He had brought me all this way because of them.

4

'Oh God, I want to be happy'

Monday morning, 7.30, my telephone rang. I awoke suddenly and lurched over to answer.

'Good morning, my son,' said a familiar voice. It was Márcio, the pastor of my church. I was not expecting a call.

'Morning, pastor,' I replied, attempting to sound wide awake.

'Son, come and see me this afternoon at two o'clock. I want to bless your life.'

Márcio was the main pastor of the Lagoinha Baptist Church, the city's biggest evangelical church, with a membership roll of over 15,000. The church was still experiencing dramatic growth, and had some 70 different ministries. The main temple building was an impressive three-tiered round arena, and I tended to sit on the third floor, looking down. I was surprised that the pastor had even heard of me.

As I entered Pastor Márcio's office that afternoon, he shook my hand and offered me a seat. He quickly came to the point.

'Matt, I've been hearing about the work that you're doing. How goes it?'

I told him of my visits to Pylon Hill, of the drug dens, the street girls, the crack. Time was running out for them, I explained. The drug was destroying their young lives. Pastor Márcio listened intently, clearly moved.

'I want the church to bless you in your work,' he began. Pastor Márcio explained how the church had recently opened an organisation dedicated to working amongst the poor and needy. The Oasis Foundation, as it was called, was looking to take on new projects.

'Go away and think how best we could reach these girls,' he said.

'Bring me a written project proposal by Thursday morning.'

This extraordinary meeting lasted less than five minutes. It was only on Friday night that I had returned from visiting the young Sofia on Pylon Hill. I had cried out to God, asking Him to do something, and quickly. By Monday afternoon I was being offered the support of the Lagoinha Baptist Church, one of Brazil's biggest churches, and its pastor, Márcio one of the country's most respected leaders. I could hardly believe it. God had heard my prayers, and answered them much more quickly and dramatically than I had expected.

'Remember, my son,' he added, as I turned to leave. 'God doesn't do things by halves. He wants the biggest and best.'

That night, I took a blank piece of paper, and thought hard. The girls were so spellbound by the drug, it was going to be difficult to distract them away from it. They needed something that would catch their attention, capture their imagination.

We needed a place where we could reach out to the girls, where they could shelter from the streets and opt out from their daily dose of crack. Inside, there should be activities with the girls that helped them to forget their cravings. The girls' self-esteem had hit rock bottom. We needed a way to help the girls feel good about themselves, to help them to dream of a better life.

As I thought, I remembered a girl that I had once helped to leave the streets. She had always dreamed of being a ballet dancer. I arranged a ballet class for her, and her life was changed for good. As she danced, she found the strength to improve, to overcome her difficulties.

Later that week I met Pastor Márcio, handing over my proposal for a 'dance school for street girls'. The house, I explained, should ideally be situated between the streets where the girls slept and stole, and the *favela*, where they smoked drugs. The house would be open from Monday to Friday, providing the girls with an alternative to the streets and drugs. The dance, alongside other activities, would be used as a therapy, helping the girls to forget their cravings. Without a second thought, Pastor Márcio gave me the go-ahead.

I began looking for suitable premises, along with Denísia, a friend, who was seconded to me from another church department. We finally found the perfect location, a large detached house on the corner of two main roads. The white-washed building was situated halfway between the city centre and the *favela*, Pylon Hill.

As we were leaving the house, having looked around it for the first time, a high-pitched voice called out, 'Oh, Uncle Matt, over here!' It was Patricia, clinging precariously to the back of the 9801 bus as it veered around the corner in front of the house. As it swerved, she almost lost her grip, her legs swinging around in mid-air. I looked over at Denísia, and she smiled. The bus to and from Pylon Hill also passed here.

A few moments later we heard raised voices close by, and then a hurried pattering of feet. Shortly after there arrived Julie, a chubby 13-year-old street girl with freckles and an untidy mop of black hair. She stopped suddenly, panting for air.

'Oh, it's you, Uncle,' she exclaimed, appearing relieved.

'What's going on?' I asked.

'Oh, it's nothing really,' she replied, catching her breath.

She made a dash for the door of the house, which was still ajar. At that moment, two policemen arrived and, behind them, a woman on high heels, struggling to keep up.

'The bitch is in there!' she cried, pointing to the entrance of the house where I was standing. The policemen started towards the door, but I stood in their way.

'Hold on,' I said. 'What's going on?'

The poor woman was flustered. She had been waiting in her car at the nearby traffic-lights when Julie appeared at her window asking for money. Feeling sorry for her, the woman wound down the window and handed over a one-real note. Julie took it, then put a broken bottle to the woman's throat and demanded her whole purse.

There was not much that I could do. The two policemen barged past me, emerging soon afterwards with the frightened Julie in an arm-lock, sobbing hysterically.

'Help me, Uncle,' she cried. 'They're going to beat me up.'

I turned to the policeman, noting his name and identity tag. 'Look here, officer. I know who you are. You have to arrest this girl. But if she comes to any harm, I'll make a complaint.'

He looked disdainfully at me. 'People who defend vagabonds like her should be locked up too.'

Julie spat in the policeman's face, and winced as he tightened his grip. That did not help my case. I knew where Julie had come from, a rotting wooden shack, an abusive stepfather, an alcoholic mother. She was now addicted to crack, and would dash around on handbag-snatching sprees with an inexhaustible energy.

The police car sped off, Julie peering glumly out of the rear window. Her despondency, however, was not due to the fact of being arrested. Rather it was that she had been intercepted mid-way to Pylon Hill, and had lost that day's chance to 'trip'. She had been arrested so many times before, she knew exactly what would happen. From the Children's Police Station she would be taken to the Children's Court, and be interviewed by a public prosecutor, who would send her to the Judge. As there were no penitentiary units for girls, the Judge would have no alternative but to send Julie to the state orphanage. There she would have a shower, change her clothes, and run away, back to the streets. For a street girl, being arrested is like turning up a 'Go to jail' card in Monopoly. It just means having to sit out for a few rounds.

Denísia wanted me to meet Warlei, a fellow student from theological college. He had done a class presentation about working with at-risk teenagers as part of his course work a few days back.

'When I heard him speak, I thought of you,' she told me. 'He was saying the things you say, almost word for word.'

I arranged to meet Warlei, and it was immediately clear that we shared the same vision. He was working for a government project doing after-school activities for poor shanty children. He was also one of the founding members and a prospective pastor of his church, a breakaway Baptist church committed to youth evangelism. As I told him of the girls on the streets, Warlei was moved to tears. Without much further thought, he rang his boss to give in his notice. He was on board.

Warlei became a great friend and second-in-command of the project. He was practical and meticulous, and had limitless energy. Over the next few years we would share together many moments of joy and of despondency. We would encourage one another through the difficult times, and share joyfully our successes. That first day, we set out with such enthusiasm, full of optimism. Our plans for the project, still without a name, were daring and ambitious.

On the streets, word of the new house spread like wildfire. The street children, always on the move, pass on news to one another at an incredible rate. It was not long before girls began knocking excitedly on the door of our newly rented white house, eager to know more.

One day, while we were still busy painting the walls, the doorbell chimed. It was Sofia, barefoot and filthy, her pregnant belly bulging out over scanty lycra shorts. I was surprised to see her, and she hugged me tightly.

'What are you doing here?' I asked. I thought that she had 'married' Tulio, the drug dealer in Pylon Hill.

'Tulio's in prison, thank God,' she said, gleefully. 'Now I'm free!'

'What happened?' I asked.

'Oh, a guy owed him some money, and didn't pay up. The poor guy ended up more perforated than a sieve! Can I come in?'

I let Sofia in and showed her around the house. As she gazed about her, she could hardly contain her excitement. We had painted every room a different, vivid colour - pink, green, blue, bright red, dazzling yellow. Upstairs there was a gym, with exercise bikes and treadmills, painted a brilliant orange. Opposite was an arts room, in blue and green. Sofia's eyes lit up as she stepped into the dance hall, a large, light-blue room with a wall-to-wall mirror and a sound system.

My favourite room was the downstairs toilet, which was inspired by my postmodern university years. Stripping down to my underpants, I had taken a brush and sprayed the room with every coloured paint that I could find. It was an artistic masterpiece, as was I also when I finally emerged. I could well imagine my Sussex colleagues discussing the work enthusiastically. Sofia, too, gave her scholarly critique. 'It's a bit like having a trip,' she exclaimed.

We decided to paint the outside of the house a shocking pink, much to the delight of the girls, and to the horror of the church architect.

'That's far too bright,' he protested, demanding that the house be repainted a lighter pastel pink. When he saw our tasteful interior designing, he vowed never to step into the house again.

The project needed a name, something that, like the house, would seem an attractive, fresh option for the girls. My church pastor suggested 'Flowers of the Street'; amongst ourselves we were not any better inspired. One suggestion was 'Meninadança', literally 'Girldance'.

Still unsure, I decided that the final verdict should belong to the girls. I found 12-year-old Kênia, together with her inseparable friend Regina, playing bowls with boulders and glass Coca-Cola bottles, underneath the viaduct next to the bus station. When they saw me, they both ran up, giving me a grubby hug.

'Have you come to take us to the Pink House?' asked Regina, excitedly. Regina, like Kênia, had lost all her front teeth, having fallen whilst riding the back of a bus. Both mixed up their words when they spoke, and often got their grammar wrong. They were like a comedy duo.

'No, but I do want your opinion on something.'

They suddenly felt important and listened attentively, resting their heads in their hands. I needed a name for the Pink House, I told them, and they would be the ones to choose it.

'Go on, then,' urged Kênia, in her pretend baby voice. 'We're good at this.'

I put to them each name, one by one.

'Flowers of the Street,' I said. There was an uneasy silence.

'That's a bit naff,' piped up Regina.

'How about "Street Dance"?'

'Hmm,' thought Regina.

Kênia was shaking her head. 'Nope, don't think so.'

'Meninadança?'

At that, the girls began to leap and sing with glee.

'Meninadança! Meninadança!' they chanted, dancing around in circles underneath the viaduct. 'That's much more better!' sang Regina.

The Meninadança Project was inaugurated on 12 February 1998, during a ceremony for invited guests at the Pink House. After a presentation from a Christian dance troupe, and a word from one of the church pastors, the house was officially opened. Two street girls, Sofia and Patricia, both barefoot and dirty, together cut the ribbon and invited people in, where we served drinks and buffet snacks. It was a memorable evening.

Every day we would go out early onto the streets, to the 'dens' where the street children were sleeping, beneath viaducts, in front of shops and restaurants, underneath makeshift shacks made from cardboard boxes and binliners. Waking them, we would invite the girls to go and spend the day at the Pink House.

Sometimes we would find them where they had fallen in the early hours, after returning from an all-night drugs binge on Pylon Hill. People would stop and stare as we walked back to the house, surrounded by a mob of boisterous street girls, who would often make a noisy commotion. It was certainly an unusual sight.

One day, Patricia, one of our young street workers, was walking back to the house with a group of girls following her. As she crossed a road, motorists waiting at the lights began to sound their horns, thinking that the band of barefooted street girls was about to pounce on her. Patricia looked puzzled, unable to understand their frantic gestures. The girls ran over the road, catching up with Patricia, hugging and kissing her, much to the amazement of the onlookers.

On another occasion, Warlei and I got down from the bus at a stop by a supermarket in the city centre. Sandra, a 15-year-old with a star tattoo on her left cheek, had been holding people up with a broken bottle as they waited, taking their money, watches and bus tickets. When she saw us, she immediately began handing back everything that she had looted, apologising to each baffled shopper as she did so!

On arrival at the Pink House, the girls would take a shower and have breakfast. If they washed their dirty clothes, they were entitled to a set of clean ones. Then they would begin activities, a workout, a dance class, or an art session, drawing, painting or jewellery-making. After lunch, there was more dancing, and sometimes a self-help group about drugs, sex or personal hygiene, or a session with Cássio, our psychologist.

Often the girls would arrive extremely agitated by an intense craving for crack. They would be restless and short-tempered, and fights would often break out amongst them. Sometimes the girls could not deal with their cravings, and would suddenly take off, jumping the iron bars at the front of the house, and catching the back of the bus up to Pylon Hill.

Others, however, talked of how going to the Pink House took their minds off their cravings. The girls loved the dance classes. They were particularly fond of the Afro-Brazilian sessions, given by Marlene Silva, a well-known Black Brazilian choreographer, who would volunteer her time two days a week. The girls would wiggle and strut about the dance hall to pounding African tribal rhythms. Warlei and I would be reduced to fits of giggles.

The dance gave the girls a natural 'high'. It made them feel good about themselves, as well as burning up their nervous energy. As they danced, the girls discovered something beautiful and tender, hidden beneath their aggressive exterior. Inside the house, where the street boys were not allowed, they lost all their inhibitions.

'When I'm here, I forget about the streets,' one of the girls told a television reporter at the Pink House. 'Inside, I'm not addicted to drugs. Here, there is no such thing as crack.'

Andréia was 17 years old, tall and docile. She started going to the Pink House every day, but she would rarely talk and hardly ever looked anybody in the eye. When she first stepped into the dance room, she saw herself in the mirror, then ran out, in tears. Her self-esteem had hit rock bottom.

Andréia was living with a gang of street kids at a place called Andradas, a hideaway for older boys and criminals. She was going out with Tiano, an aggressive 25-year-old who would beat her up on a whim. I was once visiting the gang when he began battering her with a brick, laughing as he dealt each heavy blow.

'Leave them,' warned the other kids. 'It's a personal, husband-and-wife thing.'

She would arrive at the house every day with a black eye and swollen face. Sometimes she was so badly beaten that she was scarcely recognisable, her face deformed by bruises and bleeding. On one such occasion, taking her to hospital to have stitches, I asked her why she let him abuse her.

'It's because he loves me,' she replied. 'He beats me when he gets jealous. It's a sign of his love for me.'

I was staggered that a girl could think like that, until I discovered how Andréia had been abandoned as a child, abused in the state orphanage, and repeatedly gang-raped on the streets. She did not have the slightest notion of what love really was.

Andréia would sometimes be waiting on the steps of the house as we arrived early to open up. She loved colouring pictures, and making necklaces in the art classes. After some weeks, she timidly began to take part in the ballet classes, making beautiful and graceful moves. One day as I walked passed the dance room, I glimpsed her, alone, striking poses in front of the mirror. She saw me and reeled with embarrassment.

One day she arrived at the house eager to talk with me.

'Uncle, last night my boyfriend said that I wasn't to come here to the house ever again. He said that if I came, I wouldn't ever walk again.'

'So?'

'So I finished with him. I told him that I would rather leave him than give up coming here. He just makes me feel like I'm not worth anything. Here, it's the first time that I've ever felt like a girl.'

Andréia was feeling loved for the first time in her life, and so was able to muster up an inner strength, the courage to take control of her life. As she danced, she began to discover her inner beauty, hidden underneath the bruises and black eyes.

Some other girls also dumped their boyfriends on the streets. The girls from Andradas actually left the gang, starting a new den on the steps of a city-centre shopping mall. It comprised Pamela and Glayciele, both 10 years old, 12-year-old Poliana, 13-year-old Leka, and

Camila and Alexandra, both aged 15. The den, which they called The Stairway, was just a few blocks away from the Pink House. The Andradas boys were furious, and sent me a menacing warning: I was never to go anywhere near their gang ever again. If I did, they would get me and throw me in the open sewer.

Alexandra was a bad-tempered, grumpy girl, with thick lips and a shaven head. She was always arguing, always at full volume. It was her way of not letting people get too close. She liked to sit and draw pictures, although she would never admit it.

We did not know anything about Alexandra, because she refused to be interviewed on her first day at the house. She would roam around from gang to gang, and was always out of her head on paint-thinner. We knew that she had spent many years living in the state orphanage.

One day, as I arrived at the Pink House and walked into the office, Warlei was sitting at the desk, wiping tears from his swollen eyes.

'What's happened?' I asked.

He handed me a page, torn from an exercise book. Both sides were filled with neat hand-writing.

'Alexandra wrote it,' he sniffed. 'She said that she couldn't bear to say it. Read it.'

I took the letter and read it out loud:

25 March 1999

This is the story of my life. I am a very disgusted girl. I think the reason for this is that I don't have a mother or a father. I am very angry because of this. I wanted so much to have a mother and a father. I just have aunties and uncles and a grandmother. But they don't like me. Oh God, what will become of my life? Sometimes I think that only when I die I will have peace in my life. Sometimes I sit in the park and watch the boys and girls walking with their mums and dads. I think to myself, 'Why couldn't that be me?' Oh God, I want so much to be happy, but I don't think that I ever will be. I went to the streets because of this. I am very angry inside of me. Once, on Mother's Day, the teacher at school told all the class to write a letter to their mother. The other children laughed at me and said, 'Who are you going to write to? You haven't got a mother, not even a father.' I cried so much. When will this hurt stop deep inside? Sometimes I just want to die. But I must thank God, because there are people who don't even have what I have. I pray for those people, that God will bless them in the way that I know He will bless me. I hope that I might win in life one day.

Alexandra Luiza Carmona

I also cried as deep down I felt Alexandra's heartbreak. She seemed inconsolable, lost and alone in the world. If there was any hope in her, she had suppressed it, afraid of once again being let down and hurt. Her pain seemed so profound. Only God could put together the pieces of this broken life.

5

Daughters

The girls from The Stairway were terrified. A man had been going to their den in the middle of the night, using a pair of scissors to cut up the girls' knickers whilst they were sleeping. Some of them had woken while the man was doing it, but he would dash off, disappearing out of sight. The gang was made up entirely of girls. Without the protection of the older boys, they were extremely vulnerable.

The five girls were too afraid to sleep at night. They began arriving late at the Pink House, and were too exhausted to take part in any of the activities. Instead, we would let them sleep during the day, curled up safely on the floor of the gym. I began to go to their den late at night, staying there with them until the early hours.

One of the girls, Glayciele, was a highly strung ten-year-old, with a mop of tight, brown curls. She was tiny and affectionate, childish and ingenuous. She would always wear tight lycra shorts and tops. We began to teach her to dress in a way that would make her less vulnerable on the streets.

Oswaldo, who worked in our family team, decided to take Glayciele to visit her mother. Arriving at her mother's house, he found a wooden shack, perched on the banks of a sewage-ridden brook. Inside the house, there was nothing but a portable gas-stove and a damp mattress, covered in mould. Toddlers played on the muddy dirt floor.

'You see why I prefer the streets,' whispered Glayciele.

Inside, Glayciele's mother, pregnant with her fifth child, knelt over a plastic basin, scrubbing clothes.

'There's no hope for this girl,' she nagged, pointing a knobbly finger at her daughter. 'She would rather sleep amongst the tramps than here with me, her mother. I'm starting to think that they mixed her up at the hospital, that they gave me someone else's baby.'

Glayciele's grandmother, who lived nearby, later told Oswaldo why Glayciele would constantly run away to the streets. Her mother and father, both alcoholics, would beat their daughter, leaving her black and blue. 'Sometimes her face was so swollen, I would hardly recognise her,' she recalled.

Another of the girls from The Stairway was 12-year-old Poliana, nicknamed Little Chinese because of her oriental-looking eyes. She loved taking part in hairdressing classes, taken by Dora, the bubbly owner of a nearby hair salon, who would volunteer her time for two afternoons per week. After 5 p.m., when the house closed, Poliana would stay on, reluctant to go back to the streets with the rest of the girls. Instead, she would sit and watch television until we locked up for the night. She would talk fondly about her mother's cooking, and she especially missed her two-year-old sister.

Poliana was too embarrassed to come with me to visit her mother and stepfather, who lived in a faraway district of the city. I eventually found their tiny shack, a single room that her mother rented from her sister. Inside the dimly lit room there were two beds, a rusting cooker and a kitchen cupboard. As well as her mother and stepfather, the room was also home to Poliana's two brothers and baby sister.

Poliana's mother was an upright, dignified woman, who disapproved of her daughter's scandalous dress sense.

'I used to tell her that she looked like a vagabond, or a prostitute. But she would just ignore me, and run away from home,' she complained. Her parental counsel could have been a little better worded, I suggested.

Poliana's mother made her meagre living scavenging for rubbish at the nearby council tip. Her home was clean and tidy, although she apologised repeatedly for it.

'I don't know what to do with Poliana,' she said. 'I rarely sleep at night. I lie awake thinking about her, on the streets, getting up to no good. I worry a lot.'

Poliana also clearly loved her mother, but bridging the rift between them was not going to be easy. The more time she spent away, the harder it was for Poliana to venture back home.

'Tell her I miss her,' Poliana told me, back at the Pink House. 'And that one day I'll go home. But not yet.'

One morning Warlei and I arrived early at the Pink House, and found little Glayciele huddled up tightly on the steps of the house. Her head was buried in her lap, and she trembled and whimpered. I crouched down at her side.

'Why are you crying?' I asked, putting my hand on her shoulder. She flinched away, coiling up even tighter. As we unlocked the door, she rushed in, locking herself in the downstairs toilet.

We discovered later, from the girls from The Stairway, that Glayciele had been raped early that morning. Camila had woken in the early hours, finding Glayciele naked, staggering aimlessly around the deserted street in front of the steps to the shopping centre. Once they had dressed her, she ran off, coming to a stop at the entrance to the Pink House. It was the only place where she felt safe.

We took Glayciele to live with her grandmother, who smothered her with love and attention. This made all the difference. Visited on a regular basis by our family team, Glayciele started at school, never again returning to the streets.

Richard Wallis, one of the directors of Signpost International, had come to Belo Horizonte to see the project for himself. One Saturday, we had been walking around the city, and arrived back at the Pink House, which was closed at weekends. Regina, a 15-year-old street girl, was curled up asleep on the pavement in front of the house, sucking her thumb like a baby. In her other hand she clutched a home-made pipe used for smoking crack.

I sat down at her side, and tried to wake her. She began to stir.

'Regina,' I said quietly, 'what are you doing here, in the middle of the pavement?'

Regina opened her eyes and squinted. 'Oh, Uncle, it's you. I'm waiting for the house to open.'

'But Regina, it's Saturday. The house doesn't open until Monday.'

Regina sat up, and looked at me. As she did so, tears began to well up, trickling down her dirty cheeks. Regina's nickname on the streets was Thinny, because her excessive crack smoking had sucked her to the bone.

'Oh, Uncle Matt,' she sobbed, 'I'm missing my mother so much. It's been so long since I saw her.'

She showed me the metal pipe, covered with silver foil.

'If it wasn't for this, I wouldn't be here. I'd be at home with my mother, not lying here on the street.'

'Do you want to phone your mother?'

Regina's eyes lit up. 'Yes, Uncle, I would.'

I unlocked the house and took Regina into the office. She knew by heart the number of a public telephone near her mother's house. I dialled and passed the handset to the anxious Regina.

'Mother?' she spluttered. 'I . . . ' Regina burst into tears, as did her mother at the other end of the line. 'I want to go home.'

She listened for a moment, then cried all the more, passing back the handset. I arranged with her mother to take her straight back home.

'What should I do with this?' I asked, picking up the crack pipe.

'Throw it,' sniffed Regina, managing a smile. The waste bin rattled as the pipe landed inside.

Regina's house was in a small *favela* on the side of a main road, close to the city centre. We squeezed through a tiny alleyway, arriving at a tiny brick shack, an open sewer trickling past the door. Her mother was waiting there expectantly, and hurried up to Regina, giving her a long, tight hug.

Stepping into the house, Richard and I were stunned. There were no windows, as the house was closed in by other buildings at every side. The flickering television set, its power cable hanging dangerously from the ceiling, was the only source of light. A group of tiny children sat glued to the set, watching cartoons. Regina's mother invited me to sit down.

I perched on the edge of the bed. 'How many children do you have, Senhora?'

'Ten,' she replied. 'The youngest is two, then three, four, five, six, eight, ten, eleven and twelve. And then there's Regina, of course.'

There was no toilet, no sink and no shower. Apart from the shaky wooden bed and an old cooker, the dark room was empty. The children squatted on the dirt floor.

'I want to thank you for bringing Regina back,' continued her mother. 'She's always been my favourite child. She used to stay at home, go to school, help me around the house. But since she started on this *noia* thing, she just doesn't stay still anymore. She just suddenly takes off, and never comes back. I get so worried, I'm not eating properly. It's making me ill.'

Her mother was obviously a well-intentioned, long-suffering woman, struggling to raise her children in terrible circumstances. Richard was also very affected, and suggested that Signpost find the money to reform Regina's house, thereby helping her mother and providing an incentive for Regina to remain at home.

Three days later Regina ran away from home, and was back on the streets. I found her in the playground at Pylon Hill, puffing frantically on another crack pipe.

'I'm sorry, Uncle,' she said. 'I love my mother, but I can't fight the *noia*. It's much stronger than I am.'

Later, back in England, Richard would find a family who donated the money to reform Regina's house. We divided it into four rooms, two bedrooms, a kitchen and a toilet with shower. We also put in a concrete floor, electrics and plumbing. For the first time the house had an iron door, with a lock and key. When we handed over the house, Regina's mother was speechless with gratitude.

In the pouring rain, I drove Richard to the bus station, where he was to take the coach back to Rio de Janeiro to catch his plane. Arriving at the bus station car park, we met Pamela, one of the small girls from the gang at The Stairway. She had been loitering around the car park, begging for money.

'Can I help carry Richard's bags?' she asked.

'Of course,' I said, 'but let's wait until the rain stops.' We sheltered in the bus station, returning to the car after the rain had died down.

As I opened the boot, a gloved hand tapped me on the shoulder. I quickly turned around. It was a policeman.

'Where are you taking this girl?' he asked, pointing towards the barefooted Pamela.

'Nowhere,' I replied. 'I work with the street children.'

'Why, then, were you putting her in your car?' he demanded.

'She was just helping carry the bags,' I tried to explain.

The policeman did not look at all convinced. 'I think you both had better come with me.'

We were held for nearly an hour in the police post, inside the bus station. I had left home without any proof of identity, which in itself is an arrestable offence in Brazil. I also did not have any way of proving that what I was saying was true. It was ten minutes before Richard's bus was due to leave, and the policeman was quickly losing his patience.

'I'm going to call the chief police officer,' he announced. 'He'll sort this out.'

A few minutes later, the chief officer arrived, a tall, burly figure with a bushy moustache. He looked at me, and offered me his hand.

'A pleasure to meet you,' he exclaimed. 'I saw you on the telly the other day. It's a very beautiful work that you do. Well done.'

I had appeared on a national TV chat show just a few nights before, talking about the work at the Pink House. The other policeman tried to cover his embarrassment and offered his apologies.

'Sorry about the mix up,' he said. 'You're both free to go.'

We left the police post, sprinting to catch Richard's bus. It was certainly a dramatic finale to his week-long visit to Meninadança. Richard looked rather shell-shocked as we waved him off.

'Bye, Uncle Richard!' called Pamela, as his bus pulled out. 'Come back soon!'

Kênia's mother was old and frail, and lived on the streets, underneath a viaduct near the bus station. Kênia had been born on the streets, and brought up in the street kid gangs, along with her older brother and sister. At times Kênia's mother could not even remember that she had a daughter. All day she would be slumped on a moth-eaten sofa, drinking pinga, a strong, sugar-cane rum.

One morning, Miriam, one of our street workers, was walking the streets, waking up the girls. She came across Kênia's mother, lying, as always, on her sofa underneath the viaduct. Miriam went up to her, worried that she may not be well.

Kênia's mother was clearly in a lot of pain, and Miriam helped her to sit upright. As she turned the elderly woman over, she gasped in horror. Her back was an open wound, crawling with maggots. She had sat for so long on that damp, rotting sofa that the worms had begun to eat through her flesh.

Miriam attempted to flag down passing cars, but nobody wanted to help. Eventually, she managed to stop an ambulance. Seeing the beggar woman, her back infested with maggots, the ambulance men quickly drove off. She was, after all, just an old, dying, street woman.

Miriam was getting increasingly fraught. She leapt in front of a Military Police fire-engine, bringing it to a halt.

'If you don't take this woman to hospital right away,' she shrieked, 'I'll lodge a complaint! I'll have you all arrested!'

The firemen, seeing that the flustered Miriam was serious, lifted Kênia's mother into the vehicle and took her to the nearby public hospital. She died three days later. They were the only days in her entire life that Kênia's mother had slept in a bed.

The following day, Kênia arrived as normal at the Pink House. We took her aside, breaking the news to her that her mother had not made it through the night. Kênia chatted as she ate her breakfast, took part eagerly in the funk dance class, and made baskets from rolled-up newspaper in the afternoon. It was as if nothing had changed. Alive or dead, it did not really matter to her. Kênia had never really had a mother.

Every day the Pink House received some 30 street girls, who normally would have spent the daylight hours snatching handbags, assaulting cars at traffic-lights, or holding up shoppers as they waited for their bus home. Prosecutors from the Children's Court called me for a meeting, wanting an explanation. The number of petty thefts had fallen dramatically, and many of the girls who would regularly appear before them were no longer getting arrested. Others, such as Regina, who were still answering previous charges, would arrive at the hearing well-dressed and made-up, accompanied by one of our educators.

Inside the house, each girl was a cauldron of volatile emotions, mixed with an often intense craving for drugs. Some girls would slump, dejectedly, in a corner. Others would scream and shout boisterously, brimming with nervous energy. Sometimes fights would break out between them, especially if girls in the house belonged to rival gangs. In such cases, we would ban the girls concerned from the house for a number of days. On a few occasions I had to step in between two girls wielding knives with intent.

Lurdinha was 16 years old, tough and burly. She was the gang leader at Graminha, a patch of grass underneath a viaduct, renowned for its frequent stabbings and shoot-outs. Never known to lose a fight, Lurdinha was feared by boys and girls alike. When she first turned up at the Pink House, some of the girls took off in fright.

'She's a monster!' cried Leka, one of the younger girls from The Stairway. 'I'm not staying for a moment in the same building as her.'

Like the others, Lurdinha had a tragic story to tell. She had been thrown out of her home when she was just six, along with her three brothers, when her mother married for a second time. Her new husband decided that he did not want her children, and so she literally abandoned them, leaving the four of them sobbing hysterically on a street corner.

'I remember it like it was yesterday,' Lurdinha told me.

Being aggressive was just Lurdinha's way of surviving on the streets. On her face she bore the scars of flick-knife fights, and she still had a bullet lodged in her leg. Underneath her rough exterior, Lurdinha had a kind, gentle heart. She began to arrive early at the house, helping to clean the floors and prepare breakfast, ready for the arrival of the other girls.

Lurdinha became our friend and ally at the Pink House. Whenever she was in the house, there were rarely fights amongst the girls, and they were hardly ever difficult or defiant. On one occasion, two girls, Fernanda and Alcione, both heavily addicted to drugs, began to brawl. According to Fernanda, Alcione had stolen her Bad Boy shorts while she had been taking a shower.

'You're a filthy thief!' yelled Fernanda, who herself had stolen the shorts from a market stall earlier that morning.

'You're a dirty liar!' shouted Alcione, hitting Fernanda round the face with a noisy slap.

Fernanda ran into the kitchen, snatched a carving knife, and chased Alcione up the steps, ready to swipe. Some girls were screaming, others were egging the two on excitedly. Halfway up the stairs, they met Lurdinha, and both stopped suddenly in their tracks.

'Give me the knife,' she said calmly, putting out her hand. Fernanda coyly handed it over.

'Now, you, go downstairs. And you,' she said, pointing to Alcione, 'go upstairs. And don't ever do anything like that again, do you hear?'

The two girls did as they were told, staying obediently where they had been sent until leaving time.

There were other times when differences were patched up, and rivalries forgotten. One such occasion was our Easter party, where we took a huge Easter egg and broke it into tiny pieces, as a sign of unity and friendship. Each girl was given, at random, the name of another in the group, and each in turn had to give the other a piece of the egg, telling her why she was her friend. Afterwards, we turned up the music, and everybody danced enthusiastically for the rest of the afternoon.

On the Day of the Indian, a national holiday in Brazil, we threw another party. Each girl read aloud a text that she had prepared, and some of the girls acted out an Indian scene. Finally, we made Indian headdresses, painted each other's faces, and danced a tribal war-dance, shouting and singing. Outside the house, passers-by were baffled by our noisy Indian-style warbling.

As we were clearing up after our rowdy Indian party, the doorbell chimed. It was Renata, the older sister of Jaqueline, the young girl that I had met on my first visit to Pylon Hill. She seemed distraught.

'Uncle,' she gasped. 'It's Jaqueline. She's been killed.' My heart sank.

'What happened?' I asked.

'She was owing the drug dealers at Pylon Hill. They killed her with thirty bullets.'

It was not the first time that we had had to deal with such news. Every month, one or two children were killed, run over as they stumbled over the busy roads, or shot dead as they slept, by groups of 'street cleaners', as they called themselves. It was simply inevitable that the kids would fall out of favour with the dangerous drug dealers.

There was, however, something extra special about little Jaqueline. She was so fragile and beautiful. Her photo, posing like a ballet dancer on tiptoes, had even become our project logo. As I broke the news to the rest of the workers, we all broke down in tears. She was one girl that we had so wanted to rescue, but her life had been cruelly taken away before we had the chance.

A few days later we received the news that Jaqueline had been seen in another *favela*, Pedreira Prado Lopes. I later met her on the streets. She had not been killed but, at the last moment, had escaped, fleeing from Pylon Hill and disappearing out of sight. She was already running up debts in another, more dangerous, *favela*.

Jaqueline was not dead, but she was as good as dead. Her feeble body could not withstand much more drug-taking. If the crack did not finish her first, then the dealers most definitely would. At such a tender age she had no one in the world, trapped in a desperate, deadly circle. She was too weak to react, too unloved to care.

6

Sofia's story: 'My heart is strewn with rocks'

'Matt, you don't know me, but you just saved my life!'

It was the colleague of a friend. She had phoned to say 'thank you', she explained. She had been waiting for her bus at a stop in the city centre, when a street girl came up to her, armed with a broken beer-bottle.

'Give me your money,' the girl menaced, 'or I'll slice your jugular!'

Scared out of her wits, the woman reached into her handbag for her purse. At that moment, she remembered my name. Her work-mate had often talked about me.

'You know,' she said cautiously, 'that I'm a friend of Uncle Matt?'

At that, the girl gasped with horror. She threw her arms around the startled woman, showering her with kisses. The others waiting at the bus-stop were equally astounded.

'Forgive me, please, I didn't know,' the girl insisted. 'Tell Uncle Matt that Sofia's missing him!' Waving goodbye, she sprinted off out of sight.

Sofia was 14 years old and strikingly pretty, with dimples and expressive brown eyes. Looking at her, it was difficult to believe that she was one of Belo's most hardened street girls, or that she was obsessively addicted to crack. I would often come across her as she dashed and darted through the city-centre streets, snatching handbags and picking pockets. She was quick and agile, and would slip past policemen and leave shop security guards seething. When she was not stealing, I would find her crouched in a corner in one of Pylon Hill's drug dens, squandering her day's loot in a matter of minutes.

She had been just seven years old when she first arrived in Belo Horizonte. As I related in Chapter 2, she had run away from the violence of her mother and father's home, and had at first slept rough on the streets of her hometown, Governador Valadares, in the far north of the state. A group of older street kids then took her under their wing, and brought her, by freight-train, to the 'big city'.

On the streets, Sofia quickly learned how to profit from her prettiness. She would sell her body for a *marmitex*, a ready-to-eat plate of rice, beans and meat, costing less than a pound. Her good looks also won her status in the gang, as the boys were more than eager to do her favours. Sofia was unlike the other gang leaders, however. She was friendly and charismatic, and made no enemies on the streets. On the contrary, all the street kids liked her.

When I first knew Sofia, she lived on the side of the city-centre ring-road, next to the bus station. She slept with a handful of others in a makeshift tent made from scraps of wood and plastic sheeting, propped up against the concrete pillar of a flyover. I would often go and visit the gang, all of whom would squat inside the small tent, inhaling from bags of glue or plastic bottles of paint-thinner.

Sniffing paint-thinner was a way of numbing the brain, helping the kids momentarily forget their tragic lives. Crack, however, was altogether different, making the kids feel euphoric, powerful, free.

For Sofia, however, it was a cruel illusion. Addicted on her first drag, she began to chase after the deadly white rocks at whatever cost. The more obsessed she became, the more money she needed. While the crack sucked her to the bone, her desperate need to buy began to put her own life at risk.

Her petty thieving became more aggressive, and she began to hold up motorists as they waited at traffic-lights, sometimes with a knife or broken bottle, sometimes with a firearm. She would do anything in her reckless bid to buy drugs. As we have seen, her dependence eventually took her to living with Tulio, a drug dealer on Pylon Hill, who would regularly beat and humiliate her.

Sofia was trapped by a drug that was killing her, and by a violent man whom she did not love. Now she was pregnant as well. I once showed Sofia a photo that I had taken of her three years before, when I had first met her. In the photo she was smiling, her eyes sparkling.

'I was so full of hope,' she reminisced. 'I had not even heard of crack. Now my heart is strewn with rocks.'

With the father of her baby in prison, Sofia began to go regularly to the Pink House. Being pregnant made her more sensitive and thoughtful. The prospect of motherhood also made her feel more responsible, and she started cutting down on her drug intake. At nights I would often find her alone, sitting against the 24-hour cash machine on Seventh Square in the city centre. While the rest of her gang were on an all-night drugs binge on Pylon Hill, Sofia had opted out, preferring instead to nurture her rapidly growing 'bump'.

Sofia was already eight months pregnant when I took her to have an ultrasound scan.

She was thrilled to see her baby on the monitor, and to learn that it was a girl. Afterwards, I took her for a burger at McDonalds, as a special treat. Clutching the black-and-white photograph from the scan, she talked enthusiastically of how she would care for her precious baby.

Her daughter would be called Tainara, Sofia told me, as she bit into her Big Mac. She would never beat her, nor leave her alone to cry. Tainara would never feel sad, she swore, for she would always be close to her mother. Sofia would always be there for her daughter, so she would never have reason to feel afraid.

Sofia began to talk fondly of her own mother, saying that she wanted to visit her before the baby was born. Her home-town lay some five hours away from Belo Horizonte by car, and Sofia had not seen her mother for nearly five years. She was overjoyed when I told her that I would take her to see her mother. We had helped some other street girls from her town. They had returned to their families some months before. A visit for Sofia was long overdue.

It was before 7 a.m. when I arrived at Seventh Square the following day. Sofia was sound asleep on her back, wrapped in a filthy blanket.

'Sofia, wake up,' I whispered. 'We've got a long journey ahead.'

Sofia opened her eyes straight away.

'Uncle, I won't go,' she groaned. 'I'm feeling ill.'

I left Sofia huddled up alongside the others in her gang, and made my planned trip to Governador Valadares without her. At 10 o'clock at night I was making the long trip back. It was dark and pouring with rain, and the motorway was in poor condition. Suddenly, I hit a traffic island in the middle of the road. My car went flying, bumping over the concrete island and nearly tipping over. It landed with a crash on the nearside kerb. I was not injured, but my car was a near write-off.

If I had taken Sofia with me that day, I would have been forced to do an impromptu delivery right there on the hard shoulder. For at about the same time, laid out in agony on Seventh Square, Sofia's waters broke.

Her best friend, Sandra, did not know what to do. Panicking, she smashed a beer-bottle, and stopped a taxi on the road.

'If you don't take my friend to hospital,' she threatened, 'I'll rip your throat out!'

Arriving at the casualty waiting-room, Sandra started holding up the nurses and receptionists, demanding that they took her friend into the delivery room. She was so used to being treated with contempt that she assumed that, like always, nobody would want to help.

Sofia gave birth to a beautiful baby daughter. The tiny girl was premature and suffering from some heart problems, because Sofia had been using crack during the pregnancy. It was decided that the baby, and her mother, would have to stay under observation for a further week.

Two days after the birth, I visited Sofia in her hospital ward. I waited behind the glass screen as she picked up the tiny Tainara, holding her excitedly in her arms. She kissed her affectionately on the nose, and grinned proudly at me. We talked of what she would do when she was able to leave. We decided to try and find a place for Sofia to live, where she could care for her new daughter.

A few days later, the doorbell at the Pink House rang insistently. Going to answer it, I was surprised to see Sofia, still in her maternity clothes, yet barefoot.

'What are you doing here?' I asked.

'I managed to fool them,' she stammered. 'I took the lift when they weren't looking, and I ran away. They thought they could keep me imprisoned in hospital, didn't they? Not me. Nobody keeps me locked up.'

It was not Sofia talking; it was the 'paranoia', the crack. She had stayed for an entire week confined to a hospital ward, unable to smoke the tiny white rocks that were strewn across her heart. It had finally convinced her that running away would be a smart thing to do.

'What about Tainara, your baby?' I asked.

Sofia did not know what to say. She had not given her precious baby daughter a moment's thought. I invited her in, but she declined. She was on her way to Pylon Hill.

Sofia did not reappear for a number of weeks. According to the girls, she was bingeing day and night, in the disused playground at Pylon Hill. The Children's Council made arrangements for Sofia's mother to look after the baby. A few weeks later, Sofia's mother collected her new granddaughter, taking her back to her home-town.

A month or so later Warlei and I decided to pay a visit to Sofia's mother. It was already dark when we found her home, a half-built brick house on a spacious plot of red earth, fenced off with barbed wire. I clapped my hands in the customary way.

A small figure appeared cagily in the shadows.

'Who is it?' she called.

'We're from Belo Horizonte,' I called back. 'It's about Sofia.'

She scurried up to the gate and invited us in. 'I'm her mother. Has anything happened?'

'We were eager to meet you, and to know how the baby is doing.'

We followed Sofia's mother up the red dirt path, sitting down on a wooden bench beside the house. One of Sofia's younger sisters joined us.

'I can't remember the last time Sofia turned up,' her mother began. 'She stays for a few days, and then takes off again. I used to worry myself sick, but now, I'm afraid to say, I've given up worrying. I've just given up.'

She spoke with a soft, kind voice. Her younger daughter, and toddler son, seemed polite and well cared for. Her house, too, was well kept, clean and tidy. I asked if she knew why Sofia had gone to the streets in the first instance.

Sofia's mother glanced around, and lowered her voice to a whisper.

'It's my husband,' she murmured. 'He drinks, and gets violent. He used to beat her up.' Her husband, she said, was out drinking, and would be returning at any moment. I asked about Sofia's baby.

'The baby's heart problems flared up again,' she explained. 'She needed better treatment, and medicine, which we couldn't afford. I already struggle to raise my little one.'

'So?' I enquired.

'So I handed her back over to the Judge. The baby was put up for adoption. She's probably with some rich family now.'

We later found out that Sofia's baby had been adopted that same day. Being newborn and white, she had been snatched up quickly by a prospective couple on the town's waiting list.

As I drove back to Belo Horizonte, Warlei and I were both lost in thought. How was I to break the news to Sofia, I worried. She had to know that she would never see her baby again. On reflection, having the baby adopted was probably the best thing. At least, I thought, she would be brought up in the way that her mother had always wished for.

An abusive father had spelled so much disaster for a young, beautiful child. While Sofia's father tonight slept comfortably in his bed, Sofia's life was in absolute turmoil. Her daughter had found a new home. But Tainara would never know of her mother's tragic existence. She would probably never understand why she had been abandoned in her hospital cot.

It was not difficult to locate Sofia. She was drawing on a home-made crack pipe, burning with the flame of a cigarette-lighter, hunched up in a corner in one of the drug dens near the lower entrance to Pylon Hill. She was so engrossed in her 'trip' that she did not even notice that I had sat down next to her.

I nudged her gently. 'Sofia, it's me,' I said.

She turned, startled. 'Oh, Uncle, why did you have to come here? How embarrassing.'

She put the pipe down, and I waited for a few minutes as she 'came down'.

'I went to see your mother,' I began.

Suddenly, Sofia was all ears. 'How's my baby?' she asked.

'I think we should talk in some other place.'

I helped her up, and we left the den, taking a narrow path that led out of the *favela*, arriving on the main tree-lined avenue behind it. Sofia was eager for news of her baby daughter.

There was no easy way of breaking the news.

'Sofia,' I began, still sauntering up the avenue. 'I'm afraid your baby was adopted.'

Sofia stopped in her tracks. 'What did you say?'

'Your baby got very ill,' I explained. 'And the Judge gave it to another couple to look after. She was adopted.'

It was an attempt to soften the blow, but Sofia understood very well.

'Oh God, no!' she cried out, throwing her arms in the air. 'I'll never see my baby again! She's my baby! I loved her!'

I put my arm around her. 'You ran away from her, Sofia. You left her, do you remember? You swapped her for the *noia*.'

'But I still loved her,' she sobbed.

'But what do you love most?' I asked.

Sofia sat down on the kerbside, gazing into space, tears rolling down her cheeks. A few minutes later, she turned around.

'Uncle Matt, I love my baby more than I love the crack. I'm going to give up smoking *noia*, you'll see. I'll go back home, and I'll show the Judge that I loved my baby, that she should be with me, her mother. I don't care for crack anymore. I just want my baby back.'

Three days later, Sofia was back smoking crack. She was just a child, unable to fight against a deadly enemy that masqueraded as an intimate friend, a lover, whatever. It was the only way that she knew to feel happy, even if it was for only five or ten seconds, followed by the depression, the 'paranoia'.

From then on, Sofia rarely ever talked about her baby. Six months later, she became pregnant again, but had a spontaneous abortion, her body was so damaged by her obsessive drug-taking. Crack had succeeded in stealing Sofia's hopes and dreams. Her life had been torn apart before it had even begun.

7

Blue skies

It was late afternoon, and we were praying together in the Pink House. The girls had left, and we were exhausted after a chaotic day. The doorbell rang, and William, one of our educators, went to answer.

Moments later, he returned, visibly alarmed. 'It's the drug dealers from Pylon Hill, a whole group of them. They say they want to talk to you, Matt.'

I told him to unlock the door and invite them in. They marched through, five in all, sitting down resolutely in front of me. Pedro was among them, as was Neginha, a busty black woman with dreadlocks. The others I did not recognise.

I shook each one firmly by the hand.

'What can I do for you?' I asked.

There was an edgy silence before Neginha finally began.

'Matt, we've been seeing the work that you're doing. Many of the street girls who used to buy drugs from us are no longer buying.'

'I'm sorry if you're losing your customers,' I interrupted.

Pedro chuckled loudly. 'No,' he said. 'We're not here because of that.'

Neginha continued. 'Matt, we need your help. Things are getting out of hand on Pylon Hill. The *noia* is taking the lives of our children. There are nine and ten-year-old girls addicted to crack. We can see how you have helped the street girls. Our girls have homes, but they are dying all the same. We have come to ask you to start a project on Pylon Hill, just like this one.'

The young *favela* girls, hemmed in on every side, were rapidly falling head first into the crack trap, they explained. At first, the dealers had refused to sell them drugs, but the girls would simply buy elsewhere. Some were already involved in prostitution and crime. The very drug dealers, troubled by a heavy conscience, had come to ask for help. We could hardly believe what we were hearing.

We were struggling just to keep the Pink House afloat, I explained. As much as I wanted to, we could not take on another project for the time being. But that extraordinary meeting planted a seed in our hearts, a desire to work with girls from the poor shanties who had become addicted to crack. They still lived at home with their families, but many were in just as much need as the girls running amok on the city streets.

We put together a plan called 'Dance schools in the *favelas*', day centres, situated within the shanty towns, which would work on much the same lines as the Pink House. Dance would be used as a way of attracting the *favela* girls, helping them to aspire to a better, drug-free life. We began showing the proposal to interested individuals and businesses, in the hope that someone might be interested in sponsoring our first 'dance school', planned for the girls of Pylon Hill.

The street girls who turned up every day at the Pink House were drawing up their own proposals.

'I'm fed up with living on the streets,' complained Sheilla, a dark 17-year-old. She wanted to dump her abusive boyfriend, but was afraid of what he would do to her if she did. 'When it gets close to leaving time, my heart becomes heavy. Why don't you open a place where we can spend the night?

'The girls from The Stairway were threatening to go back to their boyfriends if we did not find a safer place for them to sleep. 'In the Pink House we feel like proper folk,' explained their spokeswoman, Camila. 'But at night we have to go back and sleep on the pavement, like stray dogs. The Pink House is good, but it's not good enough. We want a home.'

Over a period of six months, we had seen an incredible change take place. The girls had started in the house with their self-esteem bruised and battered. They had believed that they deserved their unhappy lot. Now, however, the streets were no longer good enough for them. They wanted a better life, a new start.

'I'm not a street girl,' pronounced little Pamela one day. 'I don't belong to the streets. I'm just a girl, that's all.'

A safe place for the girls to sleep, we agreed, was essential. They would never succeed in leaving behind their addictions whilst they still roamed the streets at night. We decided to open a night-shelter, somewhere outside the city centre, for those girls who wished to leave the streets for good.

We found a house up for rent in a district called Blue Sky, a relatively poor neighbourhood, 30 minutes by bus from the Pink House. The house was situated on the corner of a quiet road, surrounded by a high wall, in front of a beautiful pink-flowered tree. There were two spacious bedrooms, a living room, a dining hall, and another room that we made into a dance hall, with a wall mirror. At the back of the house there was a stone courtyard with a Jabuticaba, a Brazilian tree which produced delicious berries.

The first girls to go to the Blue Sky House were 17-year-old Sheilla, 16-year-old Ana Cristina and Alexandra, aged 15, whose letter telling 'the story of my life' had so affected Warlei and myself. They had been to the Pink House regularly, not missing a single day. When they saw the house, they could hardly believe their eyes.

'I've got my very own bed, and wardrobe, and toothbrush!' cried Ana Cristina.

The girls would still spend the day at the Pink House, then return by bus to the Blue Sky House each evening, when the other girls would go back to the streets. They would be met by 'house parents' Edmilson and Giovanna, a vibrant young couple who lived with the girls in the house as a mother and father figure. On arriving, the girls would wash their clothes, do their house chores and take a shower before settling down to play games or watch television. In the morning, after breakfast, they would set off again to the Pink House.

Living with the girls was very different from being with them only during the daylight hours. At night, they were used to running wild on the city streets, staying awake until the early hours, using drugs, and having sex. Suddenly, they were not allowed to do those things, and as night fell the girls would often become anxious and uptight. The girls struggled to put their old habits behind them, to forget the street-life and adapt to living in a family environment. They now had a different set of rules to adhere to, and they had to obey their house parents.

They had to learn many basic lessons from scratch. They were not used to sleeping each in her own bed. In the mornings, Edmilson and Giovanna would sometimes find them all huddled together on the bedroom floor, wrapped in their blankets. They also had to learn the importance of going to sleep at a reasonable hour, and having a time to rise. At first, the girls had great difficulties in sitting to eat in an orderly manner at the dinner table. They would hurriedly gobble down their food, going back for seconds, and wanting thirds and even fourths.

One evening, during dinner, the girls began to bicker about whose turn it was to wash up. Arlí, a new girl, ended up hurling a plate of food at Ana, missing her by inches. Ana's plate, however, was dead on target, drenching Arlí in beans and rice. Arlí took her knife and lunged at Ana, before being overpowered by Edmilson. Differences of opinion, we taught, had to be resolved with dialogue and discussion. Taking the girl out of the streets had been relatively easy. Taking the streets out of the girl, however, was going to be a lot more difficult.

One day, Giovanna, prepared a herbal tea, hoping that it would help quieten the girls.

Instead, it had the effect of bringing on the girls' periods prematurely, all at once. The house was full of girls with PMT, getting upset, slamming doors, being bad-tempered. Warlei and I did not dare visit the house for a whole week!

One morning, Warlei was on his own, waking up the girls where they were sleeping on the streets. Arriving in a den called Oiapoque, a deserted side-road near the main bus station, he came across Juliana, aged 17, and Kátia, 16. They were both lying flat, rolled up in a single, dirty blanket. They were complaining of chest pains, and coughing up blood. They both had very high fevers.

Fearing the worst, Warlei flagged down a passing ambulance, and the two girls were rushed to a nearby hospital. They were diagnosed as having acute pneumonia, and, according to the doctor, were both within hours of dying. If Warlei had not passed by, he said, they would not have made it through the day. They were kept under observation for a week, after which we made arrangements for the two to go to stay at the Blue Sky House.

Kátia was affectionate and giggly, easily making friends amongst the girls at the house. Her nickname was Tellytubby, as she bore an uncanny resemblance to Tinky Winky from the children's TV programme. She was not easily offended, however, and would often amuse the girls at the dinner table with her high-pitched Tellytubby impressions. She had come from Governador Valadares, with her best friend Juliana, and her younger brother, Carlos, who had later gone off with another gang. At 11 years old, Carlos had already started using crack, and Kátia was plagued with guilt. 'If I hadn't brought him with me, he wouldn't have got himself into it,' she would say. 'It's all my fault.'

Kátia stayed with us for six months, before returning home to care for her disabled mother, who was living alone. After recovering from the worst of her pneumonia, she wrote us a letter to express her gratitude:

My name is Kátia. I am 16 years old. I lived on the streets, without my family, without anybody. I was using drugs, I didn't eat properly, I slept on the hard tarmac. Then I met a person who helped me a lot, his name was Matt. I was ill with pneumonia, between life and death, fallen on the street, without anybody to rescue me. Then someone from the Meninadança Project who was doing street work saw my state of health and came to my aid.

He didn't worry that I was dirty and smelly, but worried that I was in trouble and needed help. He took me to hospital, and I was saved from certain death. Today I'm in the Blue Sky

House with my life intact, thanks to God and the team from Meninadança.

I don't ever want to go back to the streets, to the life that I was living. My mother is very happy that I am here. I have a brother who is on the streets. I hope that God helps him to leave the streets too. I pray to God that He never lets the doors of the Meninadança Project shut, because they have helped so many girls to leave the streets.

With love from
Kátia

Kátia's best friend, Juliana, was moody and weepy, and prone to depression. She would often lie on her bed and sob uncontrollably, lost in a deep sadness. She was also extremely jealous of the other girls, wanting to keep her friend Kátia all to herself. Her attention-seeking tantrums were like those of a spoiled toddler.

Juliana's self-esteem had gone through the floor. She felt so bad about life that she often made herself suffer on purpose. Her mother had died when she was young, and Juliana had been raised by an aunt. She had always felt unloved and inferior, and this in turn affected her behaviour. Her going onto the street was just a way of 'proving' that she did not mean anything to anybody.

We all loved Juliana, however. She was a beautiful, sensitive girl, lovable and full of potential. But, as was often the case with the street girls, Juliana just could not believe it. Instead, she wallowed in self-pity. She believed that she was ugly, undeserving, incapable of loving or of being loved.

On the streets, Juliana would lose herself in drug-taking, a way of numbing her sorrows. Away from the streets, however, there was no way of forgetting her hurts. She had, rather, to learn to come to terms with them. It was a difficult, painful process for all the girls.

As soon as Juliana had completed her course of antibiotics, she ran back to the streets, slipping away from the Pink House during the day. I met her that night, at the Oiapoque gang, sniffing paint-thinner from a drenched rag.

'I'm a street girl,' she told me. 'I belong on the streets, not in a house.'

The love that she had found at the Blue Sky House, however, had made an indelible impression. Two days later, she knocked coyly on the office door at the Pink House.

'Uncle,' she began, her head bowed. 'I'm sorry I ran away. I want to go back.'

'But why did you go, after all the love we showed you?' I asked.

'I was afraid you were just having me on. I was missing my boyfriend in the den, but when I arrived there, he was already with another girl. I thought that he loved me, but he never did.'

Three weeks later, Juliana ran away again, this time because she had fallen out with Sheilla, one of the girls in the house. Again, we went after her, giving her another chance. She stayed at the Blue Sky House for nearly eight months, running away five times. It was Christmas 1999 when I finally waved her off at the bus station, bound for home. We had arranged for her to return to the home of her aunt, who was more than happy to have her back. She left imbued with much hope.

Fernanda, along with her sister, Patricia, belonged to a group known as 'The *Noia*-ers', as their entire lives revolved around crack. They did not even have time for boyfriends, but were totally taken up with stealing, buying and smoking. They would hardly eat and would stop only to sleep. The *Noia*-ers did not have a den, as they were always on the move. We would find them asleep wherever they had collapsed after bingeing on drugs until the early hours, on street corners, laid out treacherously on central reservations, or underneath bus shelters.

Fernanda's long hair was usually tangled and caked with dirt. After a 'beauty salon' session in the Pink House with Dora, however, it was transformed into a cascade of curly locks. Fernanda, 14 years old, had a beautiful face, liked to look good and enjoyed being pampered. But before she left the house to return to the streets, she would go to the bathroom and mess up her hair again, leaving in the same state that she came in.

'I can't look pretty on the streets,' she used to say. 'The boys will take advantage of me.'

She decided that she wanted to go to the Blue Sky House. Arriving there, she vowed never again to set foot on the streets. She enjoyed being at the house, as there she could always be delicately dressed and made up. She did not like going to the Pink House during the day, however, because she would meet all her friends, The *Noia*-ers, who would talk excitedly about their previous night's drugs binge. At the end of the day, it would take all her strength to stay behind, watching the other members of her gang as they jumped on the back of the bus to Pylon Hill.

Fernanda had managed to stay for a whole month, when we took the girls to church one Sunday evening. Each one had taken the whole afternoon to make themselves up, and before the service they proudly posed for photos in the main church square.

'I'm so happy,' Fernanda told me. 'I'll soon be starting at school. I'm going to make something of my life.'

On Monday morning Fernanda was once again at the Pink House. Two street boys passed by, calling for her. She leaned out of the open window, and the boys showed her a wad of notes.

'We just mugged a rich bitch, and hit the jackpot!' they called up. 'We'll share it with you up at Holy Mary. Let's go!'

Fernanda could not resist it. Without stopping to think, she ran down the stairs, jumped the iron bars in front of the house, and sprinted off down the road with the two boys. The next time I saw her, she was barefoot and sullied, her hair once again a tangled mess. She turned away, too ashamed to face me.

Fernanda was not the only girl who did not make it. The girls struggled to muster enough will-power to go against the flow, leaving behind their close friends and 'street family'. One of the main problems was that every day at the Pink House the girls would come face to face with the things that they were trying so hard to leave behind. Often, they could not handle it, running back to the streets, swapping the home comforts of the Blue Sky House for the cold, hard concrete.

We were beginning to see why there was nobody else working with street girls. Much more so than the boys, they experienced great difficulties in abandoning the street-life and would often change their minds in an impulsive instant. They created an emotional dependence on the streets that was often much stronger than their own desire to live a better, more dignified life.

It would be better, we thought, if the girls did not have any more contact with the streets once they had left to go to the Blue Sky House. At the Pink House, the girls were a stone's throw away from their old street gangs, and a bus ride away from a drugs binge on Pylon Hill. We decided that the Blue Sky House should become a 24-hour shelter, rather than just a place for the girls to sleep at night. In this way, it would be fairer on those girls who wanted to leave the streets for good, but who were often too weak-willed to resist the urge to go back.

It was a rainy Friday morning when I received a distraught phone call from José Carlos, the director of the Oasis Foundation, of the Lagoinha Baptist Church. The Meninadança Project was one of six social projects, ministries of the church, being funded in full by the Oasis Foundation. José Carlos always spoke to me in fluent English.

'Matt, we've got serious problems. The church is going to close down the Foundation.'

'But what does that mean?' I asked anxiously.

'It means that we're all out of a job. I'm very sorry.'

My heart raced. We were looking after 10 girls in the Blue Sky House, and were receiving 30 or more every day at the Pink House in the city centre. This news was completely unexpected.

'But what about the girls?' I asked.

'Matt, there's nothing I can do. I'm very sorry.'

I rushed to meet with Pastor Márcio. The Oasis Foundation had run up huge debts, he explained. While the church had stepped in and paid off some of the debts, the Foundation had continued to spend much more money than it was raising. There was no other solution, he lamented, but to halt everything.

Our team of workers at the Pink House had sent the girls away early, and were anxiously awaiting my return. As we sat together in a circle, I explained that the situation was serious.

'There's nothing we can do but to close,' I said. 'We have until next Tuesday to leave the Pink House.' There was an astonished gasp.

'What about the girls?' asked Oswaldo, clearly shaken.

'There's no more money,' I continued. 'We've got no choice.'

We had to hand over the Pink House, I explained, as it was being rented by the church. The Blue Sky House, however, was rented in my name. Even so, we had depended on the church for every last centavo. Only a miracle could turn things around.

The girls had become so precious to us, and we had become their life-line. It was as if we had built up their hopes, only to cruelly dash them again. The girls had been let down so many times before. It was not fair on them. We held hands and began to pray together, weeping, overtaken by a tremendous sense of loss.

'Lord, we trusted in you,' prayed Warlei in tears. 'You promised that you would bring the work to completion, that we would see the girls set free, their lives transformed. So why is it being cut short, before we have even had the chance to see you work?'

As we prayed, God's Spirit met with us in a special, powerful way. There was not one person in the room who did not feel God's presence very close, encouraging us, urging us on. 'Trust in me,' He was saying. 'Don't give up. I started the work, I will complete it. I will be with you, come what may.'

One by one, I asked each person in the group if they were willing to carry on. We would be left only with the ten girls living in the Blue Sky House. It was going to be very difficult, I warned. We had no money whatsoever. We would have to depend on God, put our very lives on the line. It was all or nothing.

'Yes,' said Warlei, firmly.

'Yes,' echoed Patricia.

Oswaldo cried as he clutched his wife Edite's hand. 'Yes,' he said.

In turn, I asked Miriam, William, Paulo and Ordália, Edmilson and Giovanna. 'Yes,' they replied resolutely.

'I'm on the boat,' announced William. 'If it sinks, I sink with it.'

We did not know what the future would hold for us, but we were prepared to give God the benefit of the doubt. If we believed in His promises, we had to trust that He would keep them. As we finished our meeting, we stood upright and confident, singing a well-known Brazilian hymn:

> Marching out in faith . . . with boldness I will go out into the unknown . . .
> I will be victorious in the fight, I will plant and gather the harvest.
> Every day that I live, marching out in faith.

8

Treading paths never trodden before

The next few months were to be some of the most difficult of my entire life. We all felt deeply the pain of losing the Pink House, our daily contact with the girls on the streets. We had ten difficult girls living in the Blue Sky House, and we laboured day and night, against the odds, just to keep the project afloat.

No one knew for certain if we would make it through. The money, most of which Warlei and I took from our own savings, was simply not enough to go round. Our workers were being stretched to the limit, some of them cycling for miles to work as we could not even afford bus tickets. Some were facing the prospect of having their electricity and water cut off, because they were unable to pay their bills. Although we were able to give them a small love offering, it was often insufficient to sustain them and their families.

The Blue Sky House, too, was surviving on a shoe-string, often having to pass a night by candlelight, until we found a way of paying an overdue electricity bill. We so wanted to give the girls the best that we could, but often that was not nearly good enough. There were times when we lacked even the most basic necessities, such as oil, salt, and sugar. At times things seemed so precarious that everything might collapse at any moment. It was solely the concern of Christian friends and local churches that kept us from going under.

In November 1999, I returned to England, spending a month speaking in churches and social groups about the Meninadança Project. It was an emergency mission, we told them, for if we did not get a major cash boost, the project would not be able to carry on. Thanks in the main to churches around the Mansfield area, and my church in Hemingford Grey, we managed to raise enough monthly givers to cover most of our running costs.

The girls on the streets did not take very well the news that the Pink House would close. For them the house was a life-line, a place where they felt loved and respected. They felt they were somebody special, not all painted with the same brush by people looking down at them as they passed them on the streets.

For some of the girls, however, the Pink House had become an easy breather from the rough and tumble of street-life. A girl would spend the day in the house, take a shower, change her clothes, eat her fill, and at night would be back using drugs in the same way. The girls were living more comfortably, without actually changing their destructive habits.

It was painful, because we were reluctant to let go, but we began to see that the Pink House had served its purpose, bringing us closer to the street girls and helping us to win their respect and trust. In allowing the Pink House to close, God was stepping up the pace of the project. He wanted to rescue the girls from the streets, and not just help them live more comfortably on them. God was in a hurry, and we were struggling to keep up.

Many of the girls on the streets left for home within weeks of the Pink House closing. One was Alcione, a tough 16-year-old who had lived on the streets for nearly half of her life. She went back home, where her mother was looking after her two-year-old daughter.

'I learned so much at the Pink House,' she said as she went to catch the bus, laden with carrier bags. 'Now I'm going to be with my mother and bring up my baby.'

Twelve-year-old Poliana, better known as Little Chinese, was in two minds about leaving the streets. She was one of the girls from The Stairway, and had gone back to her old gang, at Station Square, after the Pink House had closed. She was also back with her old boyfriend, and would hum and ha about going to live at the Blue Sky House.

Poliana was pretty and petite. The boys in her gang, suspecting that I was trying to prise her away, banned her from talking to me. Whenever I arrived at Station Square, they would become hostile, muttering threats under their breath. Without anywhere to shelter from the streets, Poliana also began to use more drugs, and more often. She and her gang would often go to Pylon Hill on an all-night drugs binge. I later discovered something that made me reel with anger. An older man from the *favela* was offering drugs to any of the boys who managed to lure Poliana to his shack, so that he could abuse her.

The more Poliana put off making the all-important decision to leave the streets, the tighter its grip became on her life. It was absurd, I thought, that I had to wait for her to overcome her indecision. She was so emotionally attached to the streets, and so addicted to drugs, she was incapable of making the right choice.

I went to see Eduardo, a young public prosecutor from the city Children's Court. A Christian brother and close friend, he would always set aside time from his hectic schedule to see me. Sitting in his office, I filled him in on

Poliana's dilemma, and her reluctance to leave the streets. I asked if the law actually allowed children to decide for themselves if they should exchange their homes and families for a life on the streets.

'No, not at all,' he explained. 'If Poliana's mother requests it, we can have an arrest warrant issued. She would be taken off the streets and returned home.'

I thought for a moment. There was still some work to do before we could reunite Poliana with her mother.

'And to take her to the Blue Sky House? Could I also have Poliana arrested?' I asked.

'Theoretically, you could,' Eduardo pondered. 'But it would be a first.' Never before, he explained, had a project tried such an extreme measure, to take a child from the streets by force. Normally, they rely on gentle persuasion, a tactic that often goes on for years.

'Eduardo, time is running out. We need to do something, and quick.'

There and then we started proceedings to have Poliana arrested. The requisition was sent hastily to the Judge, who signed it and issued an arrest warrant. The following day, the police turned up at Poliana's gang and took her away. She was brought, trembling, to Eduardo's office, for a hearing.

'Poliana Pereira dos Santos,' Eduardo began sternly. 'You have been arrested for living, without permission, on the streets. You have also been using illegal substances. This is a very serious offence, do you hear? We could have you thrown into prison.'

Eduardo was being a little economical with the truth. There was no penitentiary unit for girls in the entire state. Poliana, however, looked petrified.

'However,' he continued, 'considering the facts, we would be prepared, instead of sending you to prison, to send you to the Meninadança Project.'

'Yes, I want to go there! Please, sir, send me there!' begged Poliana.

Poliana went to live with us at the Blue Sky House, never again returning to the streets. She spoke proudly with the other girls of the moment that she was arrested.

'The policeman asked my name and then said, "You're coming with me." I was just like a film!' she would swoon.

The boys from her gang, however, had passed their own sentence. They accused me of stealing their girlfriends, to which I pleaded guilty. If I ever went near their gang again, they warned, they would kick me to death. It was getting increasingly difficult for me to walk the streets.

Poliana stayed with us for six months. She was quiet and well behaved, but was lazy, and loathed doing her daily chores. We would often find piles of rubbish hidden under Poliana's bed, or swept craftily underneath the living-room carpet. She also had an insatiable appetite, and we would sometimes catch her in the kitchen, in the middle of the night, preparing a secret midnight fry-up.

We invited Poliana's family to her birthday party, on 22 December. Her mother and step-father turned up, bringing with them Poliana's sister and two brothers. It was a tearful reunion. After the festivities, Poliana did not want them to leave without her.

'Don't worry, Uncle,' she told me. 'I'll never go back to the streets. I've learned what is most important – my family.'

Back at home, Poliana was a changed girl, so different to the rebellious child that had refused to obey her mother and had run away. Her mother, too, had learned how to correct her daughter without humiliating her. We were delighted to have helped bring a family back together.

Prosecutors from the Belo Horizonte Children's Court were equally impressed by our initiative in taking Poliana from the streets. As a result, they proposed an official partnership between Meninadança and the State Prosecution Service. It was, once again, something without precedent, attracting much media interest. It was unheard-of in Brazil for a non-governmental organisation to be officially linked with the Public Prosecution Service, one of the country's highest authorities.

In Belo Horizonte, many girls' projects have opened, and closed soon afterwards. Work with girls is notoriously more difficult than with boys. The girls, being so much more emotionally motivated, experience difficulties in abandoning their old habits. Led by their hearts and not by their heads, they try to cling on to those things that made them feel good, happy, loved. Often, their need for those things, the drugs, the sex, their circle of friends, among many others, is much stronger than their own desire to live a better life.

Our girls were no different, and found adapting to a new way of life, a long way from the streets, very difficult. Night-time was the hardest for them. As darkness fell, the girls would often become agitated, moody and quarrelsome. They complained of being locked up, unable to indulge in their old habits. Some of the girls would shout out in their sleep, or awake frightened, in a cold sweat.

At midnight one night I received a phone call from the Blue Sky House. It was Paulo, our art teacher, who was doing a weekend shift with his wife, Ordália. He was in a panic, and in the background I could hear the girls shouting and screaming.

'Matt!' he shouted. 'You've got to come, quickly! The girls are running riot!'

I left my house and sped to the Blue Sky House, picking up Warlei from his home on the way. The noisy commotion could be heard two blocks away. Running into the house, we found Paulo struggling to hold down Alexandra, who was lashing out and shouting. Her eyes were rolling, and her mouth was foaming.

Alexandra was possessed by something evil, babbling on in a deep, sinister voice. I had come across such things many times on the streets. Within every gang of street kids, there is always one child that is regularly seized by a demon, scaring the other kids out of their wits. I knew that in the Andradas gang, and later in the gang at The Stairway, Alexandra was the girl who would always go into a demonic trance.

Two other girls, Juliana and Sabrina, were also running amok, squealing and howling. While Juliana was also squirming on the floor, Sabrina had smashed all the plates in the house. Juliana also seemed to be demon-possessed. Sabrina, however, a highly-strung 12-year-old, was clearly faking it in a bid for attention. Warlei shook her until she came to her senses.

We prayed for the other two girls, ordering that the demon leave in Jesus' name. With some reluctance but little resistance, the demons fled, leaving Alexandra and Juliana in an exhausted heap on the dining-room floor. It later turned out that the girls, missing feeling 'out of their heads', had drunk pure alcohol from the kitchen storeroom. They had opened themselves up to evil spirits that, until then, had not been back to bother them.

After that night, Alexandra was no longer perturbed by the spirits of the streets. It was a turning-point in her life, in which the spiritual forces that had held her captive to the streets were broken once and for all. She still had many hurdles to overcome, many behavioural problems and emotional difficulties, and many deep wounds to heal. But she no longer felt oppressed, powerless, or incapable of achieving a better life.

A little afterwards, Alexandra wrote another letter. It came exactly six months after she had written her first letter, at the Pink House, while she was still living on the streets. The second letter also brought me to tears, for it was no less heart-rending than the first. This time, however, her words were full of hope.

25 September 1999

Hi, I would like to tell you about my life. I was a street girl, but I'm not any more. Now I'm living at the Blue Sky House of the Meninadança

Project. I am very happy. There is just one thing that gets in the way. It's that I miss my friends on the streets, and the boy that I was going out with. I also miss the drugs. Actually, I miss everything that is bad that I had on the streets, but I am learning to control myself. I miss those things, but I would never go back to them. I am going to be somebody in life.

I didn't used to use drugs. I stayed at home, went to school, worked hard. Do you know why I went on the streets? Because I don't get on with my family, because of the drugs. I started smoking at eight years old, then I moved on to hash, paint-thinner, then crack. I am very happy that God helped me in all this. Now I only smoke cigarettes, but I am stopping, with the help of the educators at Meninadança, and with God's help too. I know that God will help me be all that I always dreamed of being. This is all that I wanted to say in this letter.

Alexandra Luiza Carmona

Many of the other girls managed to overcome their 'street tendencies'. It was often with much patience and many second chances. Sabrina went to live with her grandmother after spending five months at the Blue Sky House. None of us was sure how Sabrina would settle in back at home. Previously, she had regularly fought with her family and then left for the streets, spending two or three days amongst the street-kid gangs, sniffing paint-thinner. She also knew all the attention-seeking tricks. At the Blue Sky House, Sabrina liked to boast about how many drugs she had used.

Sabrina surprised us all by never again going back to the streets. She helped her grandmother around the house, and rarely answered her back. A little later, her mother, an alcoholic and drug dealer, gave her life to Christ at a local Pentecostal church. From that moment on her mother's life was turned around. Today, the family is back together, Sabrina a normal, happy teenager.

Despite the success stories, the project was still fraught with financial problems. The small offering we were giving our workers was not enough to meet even their most basic needs. I took it upon myself to pay some of their overdue bills, putting myself, too, in financial straits. Some of the workers began to complain amongst themselves. They could not understand how, after my fund-raising trip to England, we could still be short of cash.

While the workers were close to breaking-point, the girls were often unruly, disobedient, ungrateful. It was sometimes difficult for the workers to believe that the girls really wanted to leave behind their old ways. On several occasions, we found packets of cannabis hidden under the girls' mattresses, or slipped under the toilet seat.

'We're wasting our time with these girls,' one worker complained. 'While we go without, they're just making fools of us.'

One day, we received a visit from a local pastor, Tadeu. He was humble and quietly spoken, with a proven gift of prophecy. After praying together with us, he said that he had a prophetic word to give.

'This project belongs to God,' he began. 'He started it, and will complete it. Many of your workers will leave the project, many of the girls will leave too. But don't be anxious. In 90 days this project will be altogether different.'

We thanked Pastor Tadeu, little understanding his revelation. It was 14 December 1999.

Later we discovered who was passing on cannabis to the girls. There was a gang of drug dealers in the district who had seduced some of the girls by handing out drugs. The girls were secretly meeting the youths when we let them go out alone, and some had even 'fallen in love'. The girls were easily won over, each craving to be loved, and each weak-willed when it came to drugs. They were vulnerable targets.

The girls had gone behind our backs, and we saw that they could not yet be trusted. From then on, we did not allow the girls to go out alone. They took the news very badly. 'You can't ban us from seeing our boyfriends,' they griped. The youths began to arrive on their motorbikes, rattling the gates of the Blue Sky House, demanding to see the girls. They even began to threaten our female workers, on night-shift at the house. We informed the police, but no action was taken.

One night, two of the dealers screeched to a halt in front of the house. They had come to take the girls away, they shouted. The two women who were on duty at the time were terrified. Two girls, Sheilla and Luciana, began packing up their belongings. They jumped the gates and straddled the back of the motorbikes.

'We'll be back later to free the rest!' one of the youths menaced.

Our workers, as well as being exhausted, had lost all hope in the girls. They had put their lives on the line, and the girls had turned their backs on them, chasing after a group of good-for-nothings. It was no use pretending, they told us. The girls were not interested in changing their lives, nor grateful for what they had been given. One by one, each of our workers dropped out, disillusioned.

'I'm very sorry,' said William, handing in his notice. 'I can't take the pressure.'

The project was in turmoil, and all our workers had jumped ship. Warlei and I met in a local park to discuss the way forward. Maybe we were too ambitious, too self-confident. Maybe we had barged ahead, without listening properly to God. We were certainly way out of our depth, we agreed.

We reluctantly decided to throw in the towel. It had been far more difficult than we had imagined. Nobody could blame us for not trying. I would go back to England and carry on with my life, and Warlei would find a better paid job and carry on with his.

We got in the car and drove off. My heart was heavy, and my mind was spinning, lost in many thoughts. How could God have taken us so far, I thought, just to leave us by the wayside? How could He let our dreams be thwarted, after all He had promised? I began to cry, burdened by a deep sadness.

'I think you'd better pull in,' said Warlei, seeing that my tears were obscuring my vision. I stopped at the next lay-by, and we got out of the car.

Sitting on the kerbside, we both wept bitterly. We began to pray, crying out to God for an answer, a word of comfort, anything. As we quietened, we sensed God's Spirit moving, enveloping us. Warlei began to speak in tongues, then God spoke through him a simple word. It has become our motto ever since: 'If you tread paths that no one has ever trodden, you will arrive in places that no one has even been.'

It was just what we needed to hear. God was teaching us to trust Him, despite the difficulties and setbacks. I recalled the times when I had traipsed through the thick Amazon rainforest, cutting down the thick undergrowth with a machete as I went. Treading new paths is never easy. On the contrary, it is always fraught with obstacles. But that is how new ground is won, new discoveries made. From that moment, we never looked back again.

9

'I'm a person! I'm a person!'

We started everything again from scratch. We initiated criminal proceedings against the drug dealers who had enticed our girls away from the Blue Sky House. That meant that we had to leave the district, so we began looking for other premises. We agreed that we needed a more secluded spot.

We found a beautiful house in a perfect location, next to a lake, surrounded by trees. The house was spacious, with a sizeable garden and swimming pool. The owner of the house was a Christian, and did away with most of the red tape, happy to be collaborating with the project. We made it clear that we would be renting the house with a future intention to buy.

We had lost almost everything, but had gained, over the previous year, a tremendous amount of experience. We decided to rethink every detail, in the light of the problems that we had encountered. The girls needed clearly defined limits, a stricter set of rules. The girls should agree to our terms and conditions before they arrived at the house. If one of them then refused to obey, she would not be allowed to stay.

We devised a way of rewarding the girls for good behaviour, encouraging them to try their best. At the end of every day, the girls would receive a number of coins, our 'Meninadança money'. Five silver coins were worth one gold coin. The better the girls behaved, the more diligently they did their chores and took part in the house activities, the 'richer' they became. We opened a shop inside the house, where we sold sweets, snacks, lipstick, perfume, clothes, and the like. Some of the items for sale were worth 50 or 60 coins, and the girls had to work hard to buy them. Later, we started a bank with chequebook and credit card.

Luzinete was a middle-aged woman with three grown-up children. She had been helping with a ministry of the Lagoinha Baptist Church, and expressed a desire to work at the project. We approached her pastor, who blessed her, releasing her to come. Luzinete was just the person we had been praying for. She was strict and yet loving, a mother-figure for the girls.

We called it the 'Step-by-Step House'. After a few weeks of planning and training, we opened our doors on 14 February 2000. It was exactly three months, 90 days, since Pastor Tadeu had given us his word from God. Just as he had prophesied, the project had gone through a complete change. It was confirmation that we were doing God's will. We started praying for God to show us which girls should come and live at the Step-by-Step House.

I received a phone call from the Children's Council in Mariana, a small historic town about 80 miles from Belo Horizonte. They told me of a 12-year-old girl called Ana Paula, who had been abused by her stepfather since the age of four. Her stepfather was now in prison, and her mother, who had always turned a blind eye, had lost her parental rights. It was urgent that she be taken away from her family, they assured me.

I drove that afternoon to Mariana, arriving in the early evening. When I found Ana Paula's house, a wooden shack in a deprived slum area, it was already pitch dark. A representative from the Children's Council was waiting for me.

'She's in a terrible state,' she said, taking me inside. 'She hasn't said a word for the last three days.'

Ana Paula was lying on a bed, face down. She was trembling and whining, and pulling at her hair. I helped her to sit up, but she continued to shake, clasping her head with her hands. As I took her by the hands, she began to calm down, whimpering quietly.

She was a tiny girl with a mop of tangled hair and large brown eyes. I talked to her, and she simply stared past me, without saying anything. I put to her some simple questions, but she did not answer me, unable to mutter a word. I suggested that she squeeze my hand to answer yes to my questions.

'Are you happy?' I asked. Her hand remained limp.

'Do you want to go away from here?' She squeezed my hand tightly, grimacing as she did so.

I told Ana Paula of our house, and that she could go and live there if she wished. Again, she squeezed my hand long and tight, desperate to be heard.

As I read the Judge's report about Ana Paula, I could understand how she had lost the ability to speak. Her stepfather would constantly sexually abuse her, watched by her mother. He would make her use drugs, and would even sell her to his friends. He used to beat her with a hosepipe, and would warm up spoons over the fire to burn her with, threatening to kill her if she ever told anybody. Now that he had been locked up, Ana Paula's mother and grandmother held her to blame.

I was deeply moved by the girl's tragic story. As I left her house, I turned to the Children's Council representative.

'You have to take her out of here,' I implored. 'We'll take her, but please don't delay. She won't cope for much longer.'

It was Friday evening, and we arranged for the Children's Council to send Ana Paula to us on Monday morning. On the Sunday, however, she fled from her house. When the police caught up with her, she was running for her life, dazed and frightened. Her psychological state had hit rock bottom, and she was interned in a mental hospital for children in Belo Horizonte.

Every day I would visit Ana Paula in hospital. She stayed there for a whole month, during which time she did not speak a single word. When she first arrived at our house, after her month in hospital, she was still a quivering wreck. She never stood still, but would walk around in frantic circles, not letting anyone near her. She was no longer dumb, but would simply string random words together, not making any sense. Whenever she passed near a mirror, she would try to take her clothes off.

Within a week, however, she started showing signs of improvement. She was soon speaking normally, and would sing and dance energetically, along with the other girls. At times, something would trigger her memory, and she would rattle on, sometimes for hours, about everything that had happened to her. Luzinete would sit and listen patiently.

Today, nearly a year later, Ana Paula still wrestles with her traumatic past. Little by little, though, she is being healed of many of the psychological scars. She is prone to tantrums, and she still takes a daily dose of medicine to calm her. Recently she wrote me a letter, filled with tiny red hearts. It read simply: 'I was once very sad, but now I am a lot happier. Thank you for bringing me here.'

Ten-year-old Pamela, like most of the street girls, knew the number of my mobile phone by heart. She knew that, whenever she needed me, she could ring by reversing the charges. She had now left The Stairway, along with the other girls, and had gone back to her old gang at Andradas. It was a rainy night when I answered my phone, hearing the familiar music of a collect call.

'It's me, Uncle,' sniffed Pamela. 'I'm ill. I think I'm going to die.'

I asked her what she was feeling, and it turned out to be just a common cold. Pamela was wanting someone to feel sorry for her.

'Oh dear,' I sympathised. 'What should we do?'

'I want to go and live in your house. But . . . '

'But?'

Pamela's voice became even more highly pitched. 'I don't want you to tell the Judge. Not like you did with my sister.'

Her 'sister' was Poliana, the girl we had taken off the streets with a court order. She was part of Pamela's 'street family', a make-believe family that compensated for the absence of her real family. Pamela had never known her father, and her mother was a drug addict, in prison for shop-lifting.

Pamela would often dream out loud. All that she wanted in life, she would say, was a family. She had left her home when she was just six, and invented for herself a family on the streets. Her 'street mother' was just a few years older than her, as was her 'street father'. They would protect her and provide for her, and she was very attached to them. Besides Poliana, Pamela had chosen for herself other 'street brothers and sisters'.

I had often talked with Pamela about her leaving the streets, but she was reluctant to leave behind her 'street family'. She was street-wise and knew how to look after herself. In the Andradas gang's pitch, a dusty piece of waste-ground between the train line and the city sewer, she had constructed her own 'house', from wooden sticks and black plastic bin liners. Inside, she had a neatly made-up bed, and a 'wardrobe' of cardboard boxes, where she tidily folded up her clothes. She did not smoke or do drugs like the other kids, but would always be high on paint-thinner, soaked in a rag.

Pamela adapted well to her new surroundings, and became very fond of Luzinete, who was like a mother-figure for her. She quickly shed her street habits, and tried hard to be well behaved. I once arrived at the house to find Pamela sobbing uncontrollably on her bed. She had been fishing with another girl and had fought over a fishing-rod, punching the other girl in the face. She threw her Meninadança 'money' on the floor.

'You can take away all my coins,' she cried. 'I promised I'd get better, but like this I'll never get better, ever!'

Pamela was a true believer in God. Her down-to-earth, from-the-heart prayers would always make me weep. She would pray every day for her mother. 'Lord, I love my mother so much,' she prayed. 'Help her to stop using drugs, and to change her ways, just like you helped me.' Pamela's faith was unshakable, and would often put our own to shame. When Luzinete was needing a mobile phone, Pamela told her that she was going to pray, and God would give her one. Two days later, a friend from church turned up at the house, with a brand new mobile phone for Luzinete.

'God told me to give you this,' he said.

'I told you so! I told you so!' sang Pamela euphorically.

Three months after Pamela arrived at the house, 13-year-old Leka, also from the Andradas gang, phoned me. She was fed up with living on the streets, she told me. She wanted to change her life, and go and live at the house. I arranged to pick her up and took her to the house on a Friday evening.

It was only later that we discovered that Leka had tricked me. She was a spy, sent by Pamela's 'street mother' to take her out of the house. By Saturday morning, Pamela was disgruntled, asking to be taken back to the streets.

'Pamela,' I said in surprise. 'I would never do such an irresponsible thing.'

Pamela was determined to return to the streets. In a matter of hours, she had completely changed, unrecognisable as the girl we knew, so eager to put her old life behind her. She packed a carrier bag and took off, climbing over the high wooden gate at the front of the house. She was straddled over the top of the gate when Luzinete pleaded with her to think again.

'Pamela, we love you,' she cried. 'Please don't go. Don't throw it all away.'

Pamela stopped for a moment, thinking hard.

'How will you ever find a family, if you run away from those who love you?'

Tears began to well up in her eyes. She jumped over to the other side, running off down the road, out of sight.

Losing Pamela knocked us all for six. Luzinete was most affected, and spent most of the following week alone in her room, crying. None of us could understand or accept what had happened. God had a plan for Pamela's life, we knew. But Satan had managed to snatch Pamela back from right under our noses. Weeks passed, and the discomfort and anger that I felt grew and grew. Satan had no right to destroy a young girl's hopes and dreams.

I set everybody praying, including my prayer partners in England, and declared war. I went to see Eduardo at the Prosecution Service, who quickly arranged for an arrest warrant to be issued for Pamela. When I arrived at the Children's Police Station, the duty officer apologised, explaining that they had thousands of arrests to make before mine. Seeing that it was Eduardo who had ordered the arrest, however, he immediately despatched two officers. I followed behind them in my car.

We had already discussed the strategy. I would keep at a distance, for I did not want the boys to see me. They were still threatening to get me and throw me in the open sewer, furious that I was 'stealing' their girlfriends. It would not be difficult to spot Pamela, I explained, as she was the only small girl in the Andradas gang. If they needed me, they were to call me, but only as a last resort.

We took a back route, surprising the gang from behind. As I hung back, the police car drove quickly up to the group of barefooted youths, loitering in the road which was strewn with blankets, cans and stray dogs. Pamela was sitting with some others on the kerb-side. The car screeched to a halt, and one of the policemen leapt out. I watched as he took the stunned Pamela by the hand and put her in the back of the car, speeding off out of sight.

I waited for some minutes before following on. There was no other way out but to drive straight through the gang. If they saw me, they would know that I was behind Pamela's arrest. My heart racing, I coasted slowly past where the gang was idly congregated. By some miracle, none of them saw me, or recognised my car.

Pamela was beside herself with anger when she saw me in the Children's Court waiting-room. She was black with dirt, her hair tangled and her clothes tattered. Furious at being arrested, she screamed and shouted, using the most scandalous Portuguese swear words. As she was handed over to my care I tried to sit her down. She cried, trembling with anger, not letting me get close.

'I don't want to go to your **** house! I'd rather die on the streets!' she shouted.

I gave her a tissue to wipe her nose, but she refused it. I rested it on her lap.

'I'll get the Andradas kids to kill you,' she threatened. 'Then you'll be sorry.'

'Pamela,' I began. 'You were so happy. You would sing and dance. Look at yourself now. You're thin and dirty. And I bet you haven't laughed or sung in a long while.'

'How should you know?' she sniffed.

'Pamela, we miss you. You always made the house so happy and cheerful.'

'There are the other girls . . . '

'But you're extra-special. I care about you, Pamela. You're like a daughter to me. Do you really think I'd have left you on the streets?'

Pamela glanced up at me, her dirty face streaked with tears.

'I'm sorry you had a fright. But I had to get you off the streets somehow. God's got something very special in store for you. I want you back, but He wants you back much more than I do. Do you believe that, Pamela?'

She thought for a moment. 'Yes, Uncle, I do.'

It was not long before Pamela was back to her normal, gleeful self. However, she had caught scabies while on the streets, from sleeping amongst the dogs, and she had an unsightly rash all over her body. The doctor prescribed a special cream, and said that she must not swim in the pool for at least a year. This caused her great dismay; but still one night she prayed, 'Jesus, thank you for sending Uncle

Matt to rescue me from the streets. It was just in time.'

One day Pamela decided that she could not face a whole year without being able to play in the swimming pool. She decided to fast, one day a week, for God to heal the blotches on her skin. It did not take longer than two weeks before her skin was completely healed, back to normal! Once again, God had done a miracle in Pamela's life.

She continued to pray for her mother, wherever she was. She longed to find her mother, and prayed every day that God would take her out of the life of drugs and crime. Pamela did not possess a birth certificate, as her mother had never registered her after she had been born. She did not know her birthday, nor her age for certain. We arranged for a new birth certificate for Pamela, giving her a made-up birth date, 17 April. When the birth certificate finally arrived in the post, she danced around the house, waving it in the air, shouting, 'I'm a person! I'm a person!'

We continued to receive girls, often sent to us by Children's Councils from all over the state, as well as street girls from Belo's city centre. We were the only such project that worked with such difficult girls in the entire state, which is the size of France. Our peculiarity continued to attract a lot of attention from national TV and radio networks, as well as in the local and national press.

Each girl had her own tragic story to tell, of family breakdown, violence, abuse, drug addiction. Some had been involved in prostitution, something that had become entirely normal for them. Their concepts of love, sex, family, friendship and so on were often twisted and distorted. Each and every girl had been robbed of her childhood.

Many of the girls had serious behavioural problems. None had developed emotionally in a normal way. As a result, their behaviour was not consistent with what would be normal for their age. They sometimes would cry like toddlers, wanting their own way. At other times their behaviour would resemble that of a fully grown adult. They were experts in emotional blackmail. We, however, had also become experts in our field, and never gave an inch.

It was late afternoon and I was working at the house. One of the girls knocked insistently on the office door. It was Lilian, a 16-year-old, recently arrived.

'Uncle Matt, you have to come quickly,' she panted. 'All the girls are crying. It sounds like a funeral out there.'

I rushed to see what was happening. Sure enough, Pamela, Ana Paula and Tatiane, the three youngest girls, were sitting together in the hammock on the veranda, tears pouring down their cheeks. Luciene and Deborah were also crying, perched on the window ledge. The girls were wailing and whimpering. I asked what had happened.

'I haven't got a dad!' bawled Pamela. 'I so want to have a dad! I love my mum so much, but she couldn't care less about me. I only want to have a family. It's just not fair.'

It was close to Father's Day, the girls explained through their tears. At school that day they had been asked to make a card to give to their fathers. Pamela had never known her father. Neither had Ana Paula: the man she called 'father' had violently abused her, selling her to his friends. Tatiane, a pretty, green-eyed twelve-year-old, had seen her father being stabbed to death when she was eight, after which she had started running away from home and using drugs. Luciene did not have the slightest idea who her father was, having been brought up by an alcoholic mother who had died earlier that year from excessive drinking. Deborah had been abandoned at birth, and adopted by a woman who had forced her into prostitution and drug taking. Each one cried bitterly as their own personal heartbreak welled up from deep inside.

I crouched down and took Pamela's hand.

'I just wanted to have a family,' she continued, sobbing. 'If I'd had a dad and a mum, I wouldn't have gone on the streets. I've never lived in a family. I don't even know what it's like to live in a family. I don't even know what it's like to be hugged by mum or dad. My mum's more interested in drugs than she is in me. I just wanted to know what it feels like to have a family. Oh God, why did it have to be like this? Why couldn't I just be like everybody else?'

As Pamela poured out her sorrow, I felt it as if it were my own. As I held her tight to me, I felt as if I had lost everything, as if I had nothing left to live for. I cried in a way that I had never cried before, overcome by Pamela's hurt and pain. Then, wiping the tears from my eyes, I embraced the girls where they were sitting.

'You may not have a father, or a family,' I began. 'But you have a father in heaven. He rescued you from the streets, because He loves you so much. Each one of you has been chosen by God to be His daughter! He'll never let you down, I promise you. You can always count on Him.'

Márcia, our social worker, later located Pamela's mother. She had spent two years in jail, and was now living in a small brick outhouse in one of Belo Horizonte's biggest *favelas*. She told us how she had stopped drinking and using drugs, and had left her life of crime behind for good. She was eager to see her daughter again.

Pamela and her mother were reunited at our Christmas party. It was the first time in many years that they had seen one another, and they both cried as they hugged one another tightly. It was also the first time that Pamela had ever seen her mother sober. Once again, Pamela's prayers had been answered.

'Now I'm going to fast and pray for God to give my mum her own house to live in,' she told me excitedly.

10

Anything for a fiver
(except kissing)

It was three o'clock in the morning. The night
was cold and crystal clear. Warlei and I were
working undercover, on the BR-381, a busy
motorway connecting Belo Horizonte to São
Paulo. Here, girls as young as 11 sell their bodies to the multitude of truckers who cruise this
smooth, four-lane highway, on their way to
and from the country's biggest cities.

We were posing as customers, although we
did not look at all like truck-drivers, and we
did not have a truck. Coasting along slowly,
we spotted a scantily clad young girl, waiting
alone in a dark lay-by. As we pulled in, she
came over quickly to the car, hobbling awk-
wardly in oversized high heels.

She said she was 18, but looked more like
15. She had come from a town far away in the
interior, where her father was a pimp, the
owner of a brothel. She had started as a prosti-

tute at the tender age of 12, although she had never worked for her father, as he did not think it 'morally right'. She was now working at a nearby prostitution house, but had to give half of everything she earned to the brothel owner, to pay for her board and lodging. The rest she sent back home, where she had left her two-year-old daughter. She would do anything for a fiver. Anything, that is, except kissing.

'If I kiss, then I fall in love,' she said. 'And I don't want to fall in love.'

We parked the car and went on foot for a few streets away from the motorway, towards the brothel's flickering red lights. The brothel was a Hawaiian-style house made from bamboo, surrounded by palm trees. Music pounded out from two roof-top loudspeakers. In front of the house, the street was brimming with drunken men and flirting women.

We stepped inside and sat down sheepishly at the bar. The place looked even seedier from the inside. At every small round table, men sat drinking while good-time girls, in scanty tops and tight mini-skirts, chatted them up. The room was full of smoke, and the strong smell of cannabis.

It was not long before a lively, overweight *femme fatale* bounced up. She kept fumbling her words, and seemed to have a few head problems. She was not in the least inhibited.

'Where's the turkey!' she screamed, making a grab at Warlei's trousers.

Warlei made a swift hand interception.

'Hold on, darling,' he exclaimed. I was in hysterics.

'First, tell me . . . how many girls are there in here?' he asked.

'Twenty-seven of us. And we know nothing but to give, give, give!'

Her name was Tracey, and she had come from Rio de Janeiro. When she was 11 years old, she told us, her parents drugged her and sold her to a prostitution house. From that moment on, in her words, she became 'addicted to sex'.

'Are there any girls under 18?' I asked.

'No! We're all over 18,' she replied. 'The police do raids all the time here, so the young girls can't stay here.'

'Because we were really after, you know . . . '

'Well, in that case, you'll have to go to their houses.'

It was not difficult to prise out of Tracey what we wanted to know. The underage girls were held in houses close to the brothel, which, to all intents and purposes, appeared like normal homes. When a client wanted a younger girl of, say, 11, 12, 13 years of age, he would be taken to the girl's 'home'. The younger the girl, the higher her price.

We did not stay for long, anxious not to be discovered. When I later informed the area public prosecutor of our findings, he was downbeat. He was already inundated by similar cases. There was little that he could do, he said.

The number of child prostitutes in Brazil is astonishingly high, surpassed only by the number in India. It is nurtured by a popular culture that degrades women and that often portrays young girls as sexual objects. In our state of Minas Gerais, the motorways, traversed by thousands of long-distance truckdrivers, cut straight through deprived, faminestricken regions, where families struggle to survive amidst crippling poverty. Teenage girls have been known to sell their bodies for just 50 centavos a time, the equivalent of less than 20 pence.

Fourteen-year-old Deborah was abandoned at birth by her mother, a prostitute. She had been brought up by her aunt, Sandra, a wellto-do woman who herself worked in the evenings as an escort for upper-class men. Deborah, too, had been 'on the game' since an early age, egged on by her adoptive mother. Sandra, however, was ashamed of her, for she was selling her body, not to her upper-class clientele, but on the motorways and in roadside prostitution houses. Addicted to drugs, she would spend days away from home, locked up inside brothel bedrooms, or hanging out with a gang of drug users.

Deborah came to live at our house, sent to us by the Children's Council. She was chatty and friendly, and craved attention. She would become intensely jealous of the other girls, and was prone to violent tantrums, especially when she did not get her own way. On one occasion she was caught swapping over the girls' belongings, trying to cause fights amongst them.

Deborah talked fondly of her 'invisible friend'. She would appear to her, she told us, giving her advice, telling her what she should and should not do. Sometimes she would appear, sitting on the end of Deborah's bed, or by the edge of the lake, and would talk to her. Deborah's invisible friend was called 'Rose of the Wind', the name of a known spirit in Candomblé, a popular Spiritist religion.

'She must be good,' Deborah told me, 'because she only tells me to do good things.'

One afternoon, without warning, Deborah jumped the fence and ran off. Her 'invisible friend' had promised her that, if she did, she would look after her. Luzinete and Warlei, who were at the house at the time, were taken by surprise. All they could do, they decided, was to go inside and pray for her safe return.

'Bring Deborah back,' they prayed. 'But don't bring her back the same as she left. Transform her, Lord, even today.'

They had not been praying for five minutes when a car horn sounded at the gates of the house. It was the police, and a terrified Deborah, crying and screaming.

'Don't let them arrest me!' she blubbered. 'I'll be good. I won't run away ever again. Just don't let them arrest me!'

Later we learned what had happened. At the exact moment when Luzinete and Warlei had been praying, the policemen, the only two officers on duty within ten miles, had decided to go on a routine patrol. When Deborah saw the police car, she panicked and started running. The policemen became suspicious and picked her up, taking her to the police station for interrogation. They suspected that she had been buying drugs.

When Deborah, in the back of the police car, returned to our house, her 'invisible friend' did not follow her in, but stopped at the gates.

'I no longer have permission to enter here,' her 'friend' told her, as Deborah looked back.

'Some friend she turned out to be,' said Deborah, as she sat down with Luzinete and Warlei. 'She promised me that everything would turn out all right, and then turned me over to the cops!'

Warlei began to explain to Deborah about another friend, one who would never let her down, Jesus. He died to save her, he told her, and wanted a special place in her life.

That day, Deborah invited Jesus into her life. Just as they had prayed, before the day was out, Deborah's life had been turned around.

I received a phone call from the Belo Horizonte Children's Council. They told me of a young girl who was selling her body on the edge of the city ring-road, a four-lane highway always jam-packed with traffic. Her name was Gilsele, and she was just 13.

Gilsele's tiny wooden shack was in a *favela* called Vila Moin, perched precariously on a steep hillside, below the continuous clatter of the noisy ring-road above. I parked my car on a stretch of wasteland below, and climbed uneasily up a steep flight of steps carved in the muddy slope. I enquired for Dilson, Gilsele's father, as I went.

Her mother and father were chatting with neighbours as I arrived at Gilsele's house, breathless from the steep climb. I introduced myself, offering a handshake. At that moment, a girl dashed out of the shack, pushing past me, and ran out of sight. She was barefoot and dirty, and wore a baggy knee-length T-shirt. She did not even look up.

'That's Gilsele,' said her mother. 'She's changed so much in the last four, five months. She used to be diligent at school, she always loved going to church. She was going to be baptised, you know.'

'Can't you find a place to put her, a place where she can't run away?' asked her father.

'That really depends on her,' I replied. 'I'm afraid we can only help if she wants to be helped. What does she get up to?'

For four months, they told me, Gilsele had not spent a single night at home. She would spend the hours of darkness, not tucked up in bed, but up on the ring-road, 'hitching' rides with truck-drivers. Leaving as night began to fall, she would only arrive back in her house at day-break.

'Sometimes she arrives back without a stitch of clothing, completely naked,' lamented her mother.

Moments later, there was a pattering of feet, and Gilsele arrived back, nervous and flustered. She was holding a can of Coca-Cola in one hand, and in the other a small plastic packet, screwed tight at either end. There and then, she opened the can of coke and poured the fizzy drink away, down the hillside. She needed the can to smoke crack.

'You see,' said her mother, throwing her arms in the air. 'All she thinks about is *noia*. There's nothing else. She just lives for the *noia*.'

I sat down with Gilsele, taking her by the hand. She was just a child, small and baby-faced. I knew some other girls just like her, I told her. They had been addicted to crack, but now they were happy and no longer addicted, living in a beautiful house, next to a lake. I asked Gilsele if she wanted to go there.

'Me? No,' she said. 'Why should I go there? I don't even use drugs.'

Gilsele was holding an empty can in one hand, and a rock of crack in the other, swearing blindly that she did not smoke drugs. She trembled and sweated as I talked with her. During the half hour that I spent with her and her family, Gilsele gobbled down four platefuls of rice and beans, piled high.

'She eats like a horse all day,' her mother told me.

I had seen it so many times before. Gilsele was just another young girl, gagged and bound by those tiny white rocks. Another life in tatters, another family at the end of its tether. Begging for drugs, this pretty young girl was easy prey for lecherous truck-drivers, who would sometimes pay less than £2, the price of an impure rock of crack. It made my blood boil just to think of it.

I had not yet convinced Gilsele that she needed help. She had convinced me, however, that we should be working with girls like her. Gilsele's story was repeated thousands of times over, not just in the capital city, but all over the state. They were not street girls in the strict sense, for they lived at home with their families. But, like the street girls, the young prostitutes needed to be rescued and restored. They were just as precious, and even more fragile.

Eleven-year-old Marlaine, from the interior town of Nova Era, came to live at the project just a few days after my visit to Gilsele's house, following a fraught phone call from the town's Children's Council. She had been sentenced to death by a group of drug dealers, the council representative told me. If she stayed for one more day in the town, she would certainly be killed.

Marlaine had the body of a child, but the mind of an adult. She would spend days away from home, hitching rides with truck-drivers, often travelling for hundreds of miles – and always at a price. She once stole 600 reals, around £250, from the wallet of one 'client', who later stormed into her mother's workplace, demanding the money back. Marlaine had already spent it on clothes, sweets and toys.

As well as being 'on the game', little Marlaine was selling cannabis and crack to her class-mates at school, working for a local gang of drug pushers. When she was found out, Marlaine told the police who had been giving her the drugs, and the gang leader was jailed. From then on, Marlaine was running for her life. She had 'grassed' – an unforgivable sin.

Marlaine was well known in her home-town, because she was always getting up to mischief. The local prosecutor was so convinced that Marlaine's case was hopeless that he made a bet that she would not stay for more than a month at Meninadança. When she first arrived, she tested everybody's patience. She would often deliberately do exactly the opposite to what we asked her to do. She also knew precisely how to wind up the other girls.

Marlaine, however, was quick and intelligent, and it did not take long for her to adapt to her new surroundings. While at times she exasperated everybody with her stubbornness, at other times she tried her hardest to obey, sometimes going way over the top to please us. Sometimes, when I arrived at the house, Marlaine would run and greet me, shouting, 'I haven't done anything wrong! I've been good all day!'

Her good behaviour would last no longer than a day, two at most. For Marlaine, learning to be a child again is a long and arduous process.

Recently, I was with Marlaine on the street when she saw a pick-up truck.

'I had a boyfriend who drove one of those,' she pointed out. Realising what she had said, she quickly added, 'But now I've got a new life in Jesus, haven't I?'

It was gone midnight when my mobile phone rang, a call from the house. Oh dear, I thought.

What could have happened? The girls were normally in bed by 10 o'clock. There must be a problem, I worried. When I answered the phone, there was a noisy commotion, a lot of shouting and screaming.

'Matt!' cried Luzinete. 'We just had to ring you and tell you what's happened.'

Earlier that night, everything had been as normal. Some girls were slouched on the sofa, watching TV. Others were playing football outside on the concrete courtyard. Still others were quietly getting on with their homework at the round table in the library. Luzinete, seeing that everything was in order, went into her room to pray.

As Luzinete knelt by her bed and prayed, God's Spirit began to fall upon the house. One by one, the girls left what they were doing and went to her room, kneeling down at Luzinete's side to pray. Before long, all the girls were in Luzinete's room, praying fervently, moved by God's Spirit in a special, miraculous way.

The girls saw a bright light in the room, and an angel, dressed in dazzling white. Some began to pray in tongues, though they had not even heard of tongues. Two of the girls who had fallen out and were not speaking to one another, now embraced and made up, asking for forgiveness. All the girls were crying, touched by the power of God.

One by one, each of the girls took the phone, eagerly telling me what had happened.

'God met with us tonight, Uncle Matt!' shouted Pamela excitedly.

'I'm so happy,' cried Deborah. 'God's given me a new life!'

'God came into this place!' screamed Marlaine, grabbing the phone.

'He came into our hearts!' came the shout from the other girls.

As I put the phone down, I fell on the floor and wept, overwhelmed by what God had done. As I remembered where the girls had come from, I cried all the more. Faced with so many difficulties and setbacks, I had sometimes argued with God, or even doubted Him. Yet He had kept His promises. It was not I who was making a difference, but God doing what He does best – transforming, healing, restoring lives.

As I arrived at the house the next day, Tatiane and Luciene came running up, their faces shining. They tucked a folded-up letter into my hand. Later, as I read it, I was again reduced to tears.

Dear Uncle Matt,

We are so happy with the presence of God, and of His Son Jesus, here in this house. His presence is so powerful in this place. Uncle Matt, we, the girls of Meninadança, now know for ourselves the victory of Jesus. We love you. After the blessing that God poured upon us last night, we are even happier than we were before. Thank you for all the help and strength that you have been to us. Now we know God for real, we will never be the same again.

With love,
Tatiane and Luciene

11

'I will win. I will be happy.'

In this chapter, I have given some of the girls whose stories are told in this book the chance to speak for themselves. These girls are very special to me. They are fighting for happiness, for freedom, for a brighter future. They deserve everything they struggle for, dream of, and more besides. Against the odds, they are coming out on top.

It was mid-morning when I arrived at the house, and the girls were diligently doing their daily chores. I called Pamela into the office, and she left her sweeping and sat down opposite me.

'I want you to write me a letter, about your life. It's for my book.'

'Is it so that people know how God can change them?'

'Yes.'

'All right, but I'm not going to talk about being arrested. That part's embarrassing.'

'OK.'

Tears welled up in Pamela's eyes as she dictated her letter. She lounged on the desk, resting her head in her hands and she talked.

My name is Pamela. I am 12 years old. I lived on the streets for many years. I suffered on the streets. I robbed from people, sometimes scaring them with a piece of glass. I would never have used it though. I sniffed paint-thinner and glue from a bag. I also used to beg for money at the traffic-lights. People used to give me their spare change because I am small and cute.

We used to take a lot of hassle from the police. They used to arrive and start beating us up, setting fire to our blankets and mattresses. They would sometimes take me to FEBEM, the state orphanage. I would stay there for a few days, and then run away back to the streets. I also got beaten up by the other girls in FEBEM, and by the monitors there too.

I used to quarrel and fight all the time. Always sad deep down inside. Not knowing where my mother was, or what she was doing. Missing her, my brothers and my grandmother. My aunty too, she was in prison. I suffered a lot.

I went to the streets because my grandmother used to hit me hard and hurt me. My mother, too, used to spank me. My mother did not have a house. She slept on the street with any man she could find. She was also always being beaten up. She used every type of drug you can imagine.

I got to know Matt on the streets. He helped me a lot, treated me like I was his daughter. One day I was sniffing paint-thinner, staggering around in the middle of the road, when I was hit by a car. I was in a really bad state, but by a miracle I did not break a bone. Uncle Matt helped me, found a home for me to stay. I was hurting so much, I was not able to eat or move. I only managed to eat mashed potatoes.

As soon as I was better, I ran away, back to the streets. Not that it was a bad place. I did not want to face up to the things that hurt me. It was easier to sniff paint-thinner and glue, and forget my sadness.

I became very ill on the streets. I caught bronchitis, very bad. I had never been in so much pain in my life. I was coughing up blood, had a very high fever, and everything that I ate I threw up. I thought I was going to die. I just wanted my mother, to care for me and look after me. But I was alone on the streets, suffering, no one by my side.

I phoned Uncle Matt, asked him if he would help me, take me to live at Meninadança. I did not want the Judge to know though, I told him. I was still very afraid of facing up to reality. I was suffering a lot, almost dying. I had not seen my mother for two years. I had not known what it was like to have a mother close by, I had never felt her love and care.

It was difficult for me to change my ways, living in the Meninadança house. At first, I fought a lot, always wanting my own way. I ran away once. But finally the day arrived when I looked reality in the face. I decided that, come what may, I would never go back to the life that I had lived on the streets. I was no longer a 'street girl'.

Jesus helped me change. He turned my life around. I am very happy to have found my mother after all this time. She stopped using drugs, just like I always prayed. I want her to be happy, just like I am happy. The people here at Meninadança helped me a lot. They taught me about God, how to be obedient, how to be better behaved. My mother never had the opportunity to teach me such things.

I am with my friends. I am not fighting any more, nor running away. I am facing up to my problems, and beating them. I decided to put my past behind me, because God has helped me so much. He is always at my side, and I will not let Him down any more. He always answers my prayers. Now I am fasting for God to find a house for my mother.

I am no longer at death's door, but very alive and dreaming of my happy future. It is thanks to Matt and the Meninadança Project, and God, of course. I am so happy that they have shared their love and affection with me.

As Pamela left to carry on with her chores, little Marlaine hurried through, sitting herself down firmly in front of me.

'Now it's my turn,' she said. 'How many pages did Pamela write?'

'Five.'

'Right. Are you ready?'

Marlaine sat cross-legged and upright as she eagerly dictated her letter, determined to fill more pages than Pamela.

My name is Marlaine, and I am 12 years old. I used to be a really good girl. That was until I made friends with a new girl in my school who used drugs. I also started using drugs - hash, cocaine, crack. I also began to steal, and sell my body on the streets. At the time I was only ten years old.

Every day I would go out, desperate for drugs. I would arrive home only in the early hours. Every night I would wait on the motorway, and sleep with truck-drivers, so that I could buy the drugs. I also got involved with a gang of drug dealers. I was a 'little aeroplane' – the one who carried and delivered the drugs.

I began to spend days away from home. I would 'hitch-hike', travelling from town to town with truck-drivers, always for a price. When I returned home, I would fetch and deliver drugs for the area dealers. I also began to break into houses near where I lived, stealing anything that I could sell. Then I would take off again, sometimes with a friend, and go travelling. We would sell our bodies everywhere we went.

One time, I went travelling with a 13-year-old friend. We were waiting on the side of the road, for a lift back to my home-town, Nova Era. We were picked up there by a trucker who said that he would pay 200 reals to sleep with me. He did not want my friend because she was black. I was ten years old and white, and if anybody asked, he could say that I was his daughter. He left my friend on the side of the road, and I went with him.

When we arrived back in Nova Era, he said he would pay me, but did not have the change. He asked me to go and ask where he could change money. As I got down from the lorry, he drove off, leaving me there. He had tricked me, and went off without paying me.

When I arrived home my mother gave me a hiding. When my friend arrived back home, two days later, she also took a beating. We both ran away together, passing by the house of a woman who sold drugs. We went out into the sticks, near a waterfall, and smoked hash and cocaine for two days, non-stop. As we were going back home, my friend became very sick. I took her to the hospital, and they told her that she was pregnant. But she had used so much drugs that she lost her baby there and then.

I once took a lift with a truck-driver who turned out to be smuggling drugs. He took me to a motel, and we smoked all kinds of drugs there. He paid me 100 reals, and also gave me some dope and some crack. I hid the drugs near my house, and every day I went there with a friend to smoke. I smoked so much that I became ill, and arrived back home throwing up. That was when my mother found out that I was using drugs.

My mother went to the Judge and told him about the woman who was selling me the drugs. The police went and arrested the woman, and she denied everything in front of the prosecutor. So they raided her house. They found boxes of drugs, and even guns and hand grenades. She was sentenced to three years in jail. The rest of the gang said that they would find me and kill me.

The Judge said that I would go and live in a convent. I was relieved when it turned out to be here at Meninadança! The prosecutor even made a bet that I would not stay, because I have never managed to stay in one place for very long.

At Meninadança my life was changed. Here, I learned about what is right and wrong. I am getting to know the Word of God. I feel that I am a better person, and that I do not need drugs to be happy. Drugs only lead to sadness and despair. I am ashamed that I used my body to make money. But I know that God has made me a new person.

I want my family by my side. I am not finding leaving behind the drugs difficult. But I fear for the safety of my family, because of the trouble I made for them. I do not want to know about drugs anymore. Now, I want peace and a different life. My dream is to be rich, but with money earned worthily.

Marlaine's story had filled seven pages, two more than Pamela's. She skipped off happily to boast.

'Don't tell my mum, will you?' she shouted back. 'She'd kill me!'

Kátia, known to us all as Tellytubby, rang me out of the blue. It had been over a year since she had left the Blue Sky House, going back to her home-town to live with her disabled mother. She had come back now, she told me, along with her mother, to find her 13-year-old brother, who had been missing ever since Kátia first arrived with him on the streets of Belo Horizonte.

'How are you?' I asked.

'I'm well,' she replied. 'I'm missing you all, though. But I know that I have to stay with my mum. She needs me.'

I asked Kátia if she would write a letter about her life for my book. We later met at an underground station where I bought her a pizza, and she handed over the scribbled page that she had written.

Here I am going to tell you about how my life changed after I got to know the Meninadança Project. I ran away from my mother's house, along with my younger brother and my best friend, Juliana. We took the train to Belo Horizonte. I was fed up with living at home, I wanted some adventure. Now I feel ashamed of what I did, without thinking of my mother's health, or of what could happen to my brother. He is still on the streets today.

It was not long before I was trapped, addicted to drugs, suffering a lot. I walked aimlessly around the streets, lost and hungry. There was nothing to eat, and I could not bring myself to steal like the other kids did. My brother, too, began to use crack with another gang. I have not seen him since.

I began to get very afraid. The place where I was staying on the streets was getting very violent. One day, a man arrived and stabbed a boy in the back, right next to me. I also began to get very ill, not eating properly, sleeping out in the cold. I caught pneumonia and could not even move, the pain was so great. I thought that I was going to die.

It was at that moment, when I was on the brink of death, that God sent the workers from the Meninadança Project to help me. From then on my life began to change. I went to live at the Blue Sky House, where I learned so many things that I remember even today. I learned how to live in society, and how to accept myself the way that I am. I learned that the street is not a home for anybody. I learned the importance of my family.

Today, thanks to God, I have left the streets and live very happily with my family. I never want to go back to the life that I lived. I am back at school, trying to make a better life for myself, and for my mother. My dream is to get married and have my own family, to be somebody in life.

I hope that, just like me, the other girls that are still on the streets can also be helped to leave the drugs behind, and have a new life. Today, I do not use drugs. I am free from this, and very happy.

I had not heard from Sofia for months, nor seen her sprinting about the city streets on one of her escapades of drug-induced thieving. Then, as I was writing this chapter, she rang me. She had been arrested and sent to a new detention centre for girls, where she had spent the last four months. It was Monday, the day the girls were allowed to make their weekly phone call. She was pregnant again, she told me, and almost due. She asked me to pay her a visit, and to take a box of chocolates, her 'craving'.

Wednesday was visiting day at the São Jerônimo Centre for Social Re-Education. Sofia smiled as she saw me, hobbled up and gave me a hug. She was not the same girl as the one I had known on the streets. She looked happy and healthy, and talked calmly and quietly.

'It's really good to see you, Sofia,' I said.

'Please, Uncle, don't call me Sofia,' she replied. 'It's Gislaine, that's my real name. Sofia was my nickname, my street name. I don't want to remember the streets anymore.'

Being arrested, she told me, was the best thing that could have happened to her. She had spent four months free from drugs. It was time enough for her to reflect on her life, and to consider the life of her new baby, Bruno.

'I regret so much running away from my baby daughter,' she said. 'I don't want to lose another baby. I won't let crack ruin my life again, I really won't.'

A week later, Sofia gave birth to a beautiful, healthy baby son. I went to visit her in hospital, and watched as she doted over him, smothering him with motherly love. Sofia held him tenderly in her arms, dictating her letter as I wrote.

My name is Gislaine. My name used to be Sofia, before I left the streets. I lived on the streets for many years, since the age of six. I ran away from home because my father used to beat up my mother, and beat me up as well. I became bitter, revolted with my life. I left my home and went into the world, at just six years old. At first, I stayed on the streets of my home town, Governador Valadares, sniffing paint-thinner.

My mother went and found me on the streets, and took me home. But my father carried on beating me up, so I ran away again. This time I went to Vitória. It was a big city, near the sea. I got to know the street kids there, and they taught me how to smoke cannabis. I was seven years of age. From there, I took the train to Belo Horizonte.

It was in Belo Horizonte that I began to steal. The other kids egged me on. I used the money to buy food and cannabis. Then I learned how to smoke crack. The first time I smoked crack, I felt on top of the world. But only for the first time.

Smoking crack made me want to steal more and more. Everything for crack. I became completely addicted. I could not stop myself. My life was out of control. I would steal 100, 200, 300 reals a day, and spend it all on crack. Sometimes I would buy clothes for myself, but I could not manage to keep the clothes. I would sell them all and buy crack.

Crack was a big illusion. It made me paranoid, afraid, petrified. When I was smoking it, I would think that the police were coming to get me. After I came down, I would become desperate to smoke more. I would sell anything, my clothes, my shoes, jewellery, whatever I had. After I had sold everything, I would go back into the city to steal. I thought that I would always be like this, that crack would not do me any harm.

Crack did not let me keep my daughter. I walked away from her, because of the drugs. I lost another baby when I was four months pregnant. I smoked drugs, without stopping, in the hot sun. I became ill, and lost my baby.

Never again will I let crack ruin my life, steal my happiness. I will never let my baby go. Only when he gets married. I will keep him close to me until then.

I lost my childhood and my adolescence on the streets. There is nothing good about the streets, nothing at all. If there were, I would still be there today. After I started using crack, my life got worse and worse. I was only interested in smoking and stealing. Nothing else mattered, not even my own flesh and blood.

I want to build a better life for myself. Before, I was always ill, always gasping for air. Now, I feel well. I am breathing and sleeping properly. Before, I would hardly sleep at all. I thank Uncle Matt for all the love he has shown me. He would go into the drug den at Holy Mary and find me, tell me that God could help me. No one else had the courage to do that. I am sure that, now, things will work out for me.

Later, Sofia passed on a poem that she had written. She had begun to learn to read and write while in the detention centre. It went:

To be young is to live life to the full,
To not be afraid of trying,
To build a happy future, full of hope.
It is to make of the obstacles
Steps on the stairway to success.
I will win. I will be happy.

12

The scent of water

There was no use hoping. Any glimmer of hope had long faded. Four days ago, Mary's brother had been taken ill and died. It was so sudden, it was hard for his family and friends to take in. There was no one who was not fond of Mary's brother.

Mary and her younger sister wept bitterly as the loss of their precious brother sank in. Friends came from miles around the town to share in their grieving, and to say their final goodbyes. Even after four days, when his body had begun to reek in the heat, people were still flocking to the tomb, eager to pay their last respects. One of them was a dear friend of Mary's brother, and was known to perform miracles. His name was Jesus.

Mary's sister, Martha, ran out to meet Jesus as He arrived, tired from the long journey on foot to Bethany.

'Why didn't you come earlier?' she sobbed, her face streaked with tears. 'If you'd have been here when he got ill, you could have saved him.'

'Don't worry,' comforted Jesus. 'Your brother will live again.'

Martha did not understand, and cried all the more. 'I know that he will go to heaven, and that one day I'll see him. But it doesn't stop the pain.'

Mary, dressed all in black and surrounded by the hysterical wailing of hired mourners, came out of the house and fell on the dusty ground at Jesus' feet.

'If you'd been here, my dear brother would not have died,' she sobbed.

Jesus looked around, contemplating the tragic scene before Him. Mary's brother, Lazarus, was laid in a hillside tomb, the entrance sealed by a huge stone slab. All around, people wept and wailed, seized by grief and hopelessness. Tears began to well up, spilling down Jesus' cheeks, wetting the dusty dry soil.

'Look,' said one mourner. 'Jesus loved him too.'

They thought that He, too, had lost all hope. But Jesus was not touched by grief, nor hopelessness. He was the Resurrection and the Life. Lazarus' death was not an occasion for mourning, but rather an opportunity for Jesus to prove his death-defying power. Little did they know it. At the Master's call, Lazarus staggered out, wrapped from head to toe in grave clothes. Raised from death, restored to life.

A beautiful young girl lay stretched out hopelessly on the busy corner of one of the city's main streets. Asleep, knocked out by her daily overdose of crack, she lay dangerously close to the kerbside. Her jet-black hair, caked in dirt, draped into the gutter, where buses and taxis screeched past. She lay open-mouthed, her lips broken and bleeding, her fragile body sucked to the bone. She wore a white, frilly dress.

I watched as the rush-hour crowd negotiated its way around her. One smartly dressed man, not looking where he was stepping, trod in the tiny girl's hair. Another woman, laden with shopping bags, tripped over her foot, muttering in disgust as she went. Others stepped over her or hurried around her, as if she were nothing but an inanimate object, thrown thoughtlessly there, on the busy street corner.

I went over and helped the girl up.

'You can't stay here,' I told her. 'You're too near the road, and the sun is scorching.'

As I crouched on the ground, holding her feeble, exhausted body in my arms, passers-by stopped in their tracks, open-mouthed. They had never seen anyone soil his shirt to pick up a street girl. I put her to lie down again in a shady corner, underneath a closed shop-front, away from the crowd and the cars. Some shook their heads despondently, and walked on.

The street girl, for many, is an unsolvable problem, a hopeless case, a useless cause. Just as with Mary's brother, four days dead, wrapped up in grave clothes, laid in a dark tomb, sealed in with a heavy stone, it is not even worth reaching out or getting near, for she will never be revived, restored to life. And besides, there is a terrible smell. All around, people look on, filled with pity and sadness, just like that bleak crowd at Bethany, where the wailing mourners did not expect a miracle even from Jesus.

I remember the feeling of utter hopelessness, as I sat with the girls as they puffed desperately on their crack pipes, one rock after the other. I could hardly keep the tears from welling up and bursting out. There seemed no way out for them. Their grave clothes were too tightly wrapped, their tombstones too heavy to budge. All signs of life had faded away. I felt so useless, as if time had long run out. Then I heard the voice of Jesus, saying to me, 'Look through my eyes, not through yours.'

As Jesus looked upon the weeping crowd at Bethany, He also cried. His tears, though, were not of despair, nor of sadness, nor hopelessness. Jesus does not look with pity, but with compassion. There is a fundamental difference. Whoever looks with pity says, 'That's terrible,' and walks on, forgetting it all in that same instant. Whoever looks with compassion is never able to walk on, forget, or ignore. That person says, 'That's terrible. I cannot allow this to happen.'

It was compassion that moved Jesus to go to the dark, death-ridden tomb, calling out 'Lazarus!', transforming the cries of mourning and misery into tears of joy. It was compassion that led Him to my tomb and yours, calling us by name. For 'God, who is rich in mercy, made us alive with Christ even when we were dead in transgressions.' If we want to follow Jesus, we must look at the world with *compassion*.

If there is one thing that motivates me, and those who work with me, it is the certainty that Jesus is able to raise the dead. He specialises in taking broken, irreparable lives, turning them around, giving them a brand new life. He makes all things new, breathes his life-giving breath. It is what He does best.

Today, Jesus looks at the street girl and cries, in the same way that He looked at Lazarus' hillside tomb, His heart filled with compassion. Looking through Jesus' eyes, I can never walk away, forget or ignore her. Looking through Jesus' eyes, I begin to love her in the way that God does. Her pain becomes my pain, her tragedy my tragedy. Looking through Jesus' eyes, I can never, ever lose hope. She is not a lost soul, a hopeless case, but an opportunity for God to demonstrate His power.

Just as Jesus touched the lepers and welcomed the outcasts, so must we. Just as He identified with the poor and the weak, so must we. He calls us to put our lives on the line for the suffering, the vulnerable, the victims of injustice. Loving the unloved is not just an optional extra. It is the heart and soul of the Christian gospel.

Jesus did not mince words, yet even today many of His followers fail to understand. 'Whatever you do for the least of these, you do for me,' he said. He is saying that, if we claim to love Him, we have to love them, the despised and downtrodden. To do this is not just to obey Christ. It is to minister to Christ Himself.

To each of us who profess to serve Him, Jesus looks us in the eyes and asks, 'How much do you love me? You say that you love me, you sing that you love me. But how much do you really love me? For I am out there on the streets, lost and lonely, lying in the gutter. I am being beaten and abused, robbed of my childhood. I am selling my body on the street corner, I am locked in a brothel bedroom. I am violent, despised, disposable. Do you really love me as much as you say? Then prove it.'

As I write this final chapter, my heart is over-flowing with hope. I have just returned from taking Sofia and her new-born son to live with the family of the baby's father. I cannot describe the emotion I felt, seeing her settling down happily, so in love with her beautiful baby son.

'I don't want ever to see a rock of crack again as long as I live,' she said to me as I walked her out of the hospital. 'I love my baby too much. I don't want to lose him.'

I helped Sofia as she bathed her baby. She treated him so delicately, so tenderly, three days old, so tiny and fragile. I doted over both of them, my heart bursting. I recalled how, four years ago, I told a fellow street worker that one day I would take Sofia off the streets.

'Never!' he laughed. 'She's the worst of them all. You're wasting your time.'

I remember how I fought to keep back the tears, seeing Sofia fast asleep on the kerbside, her beautiful face pale and lifeless. And the times that I sat with her, in the disused play-ground on Pylon Hill, her life going up in a puff of smoke. I have been with her at every moment, as her life went from bad to worse.

'Forget Sofia,' many told me. 'She is a lost cause.'

But I could never give up hope. I knew that, somehow, God would one day restore Sofia to life. As I write, the tears are rolling down my cheeks. God brought her back from the dead, just as He raised the rotting Lazarus. For me, the raising of Sofia is just as miraculous, if not more so. Thank you, Lord, for your death-defying power!

The last few years of my life have been a roller-coaster ride, breathtaking and exciting. But through all the ups and downs, I have learned something that is now lodged deep in my soul, something about which no one will ever convince me otherwise: there is hope.

Job 14:7 tells us that when a tree is cut down, there is always hope that it will sprout again and produce new branches: 'Its roots may grow old in the ground and its stump die in the soil, yet at the scent of water it will bud and put forth shoots like a plant.' We need to be that 'scent of water', bringing hope and life, the life of Christ, to a dying world.

At the lakeside house we continue to see God reviving and restoring the broken lives of our young girls. Here, they are finding love and security, a family and a future. Most of all, they are each coming to know God as their father and as their friend. It is so good to see how their lives are being turned around.

We will soon be starting our first dance school, in Belo Horizonte's biggest slum, the *favela* Pedreira Prado Lopes. Using dance as a method to reach people, we will be working with over 200 teenage girls who live in the *favela* and are exposed to every kind of urban-social problem imaginable. Although not living on the streets, many are victims of violence, the drug culture, domestic abuse and sexual exploitation, as well as perhaps the most debilitating of them all - prejudice. We have plans to start such 'slum dance schools' in every major *favela* in the city, including Pylon Hill.

Our Meninadança Parents' Association is all but up and running. It is a means through which we are able to advise and help the mothers and fathers of the street girls. As well as being a self-help group for those involved, almost all mothers, we are also teaching them how to be better, more responsible, parents.

Alongside the Children's Councils of two municipalities, through which pass the main interstate highways, we are launching our Campaign Against the Abusive Lift, targeting truck-drivers who pick up underage girls for sex. Besides a high-profile billboard and leafleting campaign, an army of volunteers will be on night patrol along the length of the two principal motorways.

We also plan to start a number of residential homes, small family units of house parents and four girls, where the girls can go to live if, after their period of recuperation, they cannot, for whatever reason, return to live with their families. The homes would promote a normal, family environment, helping the girls to integrate fully back into society.

We continue to dream, and continue to trust in God for His provision. While we lack resources, money and workers, we have never lacked enthusiasm. God is in control, and will provide, we know, although we still lose patience at times. We are determined to march on, come what may, 'treading paths never trodden before'.

The night is cool and crystal clear. I am alone, at one of my favourite spots, high up on the hillside. From here, I can see the entire city, a breathtaking sight. I often come here. It is like sitting in front of a massive cinema screen, awash with millions of tiny flickering lights - the towering downtown skyscrapers, colourful illuminated billboards, the four-lane ring-road, thousands of minuscule cars moving slowly along. From far up here, it all seems so quiet, so calm.

From up here, the *favelas* twinkle like Christmas trees, or clusters of flickering fireflies. The city streets look clean and pretty. Towering behind, silhouetted in the starry night sky, the famous mountain range that gave Belo Horizonte its name, Beautiful Horizon. This city is 100 years old, and home to some four million people. I have become involved in the lives of just a few of them.

I gaze over the glistening city, and am filled with love for it. So many suffering children, their childhoods torn apart, so much pain, so much injustice. So many lost opportunities, so many broken marriages, so many beaten wives, so many tormented sons and daughters. Children ending up with a bullet in the head, or dying from a deadly dose of drugs. So many young girls, being abused for the hundredth, two-hundredth time. So little future, so much darkness.

But there is hope, because Jesus lives. And while He lives, there is hope. For the streets girls, for me, for you.

STRATEGIC GLOBAL ASSISTANCE, INC.
2601 Benham Ave.
Elkhart, IN 46517

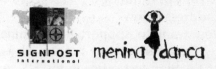

Signpost International
and the
Meninadança Project

The Meninadança Project works with street girls and at-risk girls in Belo Horizonte, one of Brazil's biggest cities. Its aim is to rescue and restore girls who are victims of 'social violence', living on the streets, addicted to drugs, involved in prostitution or victims of domestic violence and sexual abuse.

Meninadança is a project of Signpost International, a UK registered charity working to share the gospel in word and action with children and families at risk. Established in 1993, Signpost now works in Brazil, Uganda, Rwanda, the Philippines and Russia with some of the world's poorest people. They provide many short-term opportunities for those who wish to join hands with the needy and suffering around the world. If you would like to know more about Signpost International and its projects, as well as information on short-term opportunities, please get in touch at the address below.

If you want to support the Meninadança Project, financially or in prayer, please also contact the Signpost office in the UK, or send an e-mail to meninadanca@signpost-international.org. You can get in touch with Matt Roper at matt@signpost-international.org and you can visit the Meninadança website, at www. meninadanca.org.

Signpost International
Chapel House
Chapel Lane
St. Ives
Huntingdon
Cambridgeshire
PE27 5DX. Tel. 01480 380074
enquiries@signpost-international.org
www.signpost-international.org

Signpost International is a designated charity of

menina dança

www.street-girls.org

Street Girls is an interactive book. Accessing the book's website, www.street-girls.org, you will be able to see pictures of the girls whose stories are told in this book, chapter by chapter. After you have read each chapter, enter online, answer a simple question, and you can see the pictures! You can also post your own message for other readers, as well as finding out how you can help change more lives.